ISBN 978-1-330-88162-0
PIBN 10116522

This book is a reproduction of an important historical work. Forgotten Books uses state-of-the-art technology to digitally reconstruct the work, preserving the original format whilst repairing imperfections present in the aged copy. In rare cases, an imperfection in the original, such as a blemish or missing page, may be replicated in our edition. We do, however, repair the vast majority of imperfections successfully; any imperfections that remain are intentionally left to preserve the state of such historical works.

For support please visit www.forgottenbooks.com

1 MONTH OF FREE READING

at

www.ForgottenBooks.com

By purchasing this book you are eligible for one month membership to ForgottenBooks.com, giving you unlimited access to our entire collection of over 1,000,000 titles via our web site and mobile apps.

To claim your free month visit: www.forgottenbooks.com/free116522

COUNTRY CURATE'S

AUTOBIOGRAPHY:

OR PASSAGES OF

A LIFE WITHOUT A LIVING.

Curo—curas—curavi.
Var. Lect.
Curo—curavi—curas

(Translation,)
Cares are my lot, and cares have ever been—
A Curate I—

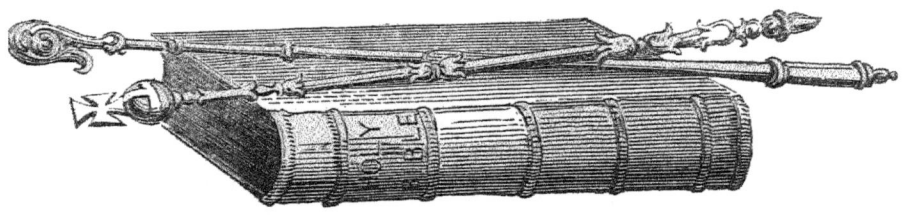

IN TWO VOLUMES.

VOL. I.

LONDON:

SMITH, ELDER AND CO. CORNHILL,

BOOKSELLERS TO THEIR MAJESTIES.

1836.

LONDON:

PRINTED BY STEWART AND CO.
OLD BAILEY.

PREFACE.

AN AUTOBIOGRAPHY, even when it carries with it the sanction of personage or celebrity, labours under a reproach which it must always require a good deal of moral courage to encounter. A man, say they, must needs have a considerable share of self-conceit or ill humour, before he can sit down, day by day, and write about himself; as if he thought his thoughts more profound, and judged his judgment more worthy, than what we see to distinguish every moral creature in the universe.

One thing, however, is certain—that, if all writers had been restrained from this mode of *renowning* (as the German students have it), literature would be minus her most fascinating smile: for there is, after all the odium cast upon it, a something so endearing in the *first person singular*, that it carries one along with it just as a shadow follows the substance, encouraging us with a show of reality and rewarding us with the consolation of (at least, apparent) truth.

Though the writer of the following pages is too insignificant to be accountable to any earthly being, he nevertheless feels called upon, here, *in limine*, to give a reason of the undertaking, and to state, at once, what is the *operis occasio* which has prompted him to take his place at the *fag-end* of those who have written some portion of the lives of themselves.

It is this: The Church has many enemies, —these are not dreaded; but she has, also, many friends, no small portion of whom are negatively hostile to her cause. While those are roaring without, these are snoring within; and it is difficult to say which most offends the tranquil spirit of the religion of peace. It is just to say a word of caution that the author ventures from his obscurity; and if the exhibition of a few *things as they are*, with reference to the church, be worth attention, here-follows the "unvarnished tale."

October 15, 1836.

CONTENTS.

VOLUME THE FIRST.

CHAPTER I.

CHAPTER II.

CHAPTER VII.

CHAPTER VIII.

CHAPTER IX.

CHAPTER X.

CHAPTER XI.

CHAPTER XII.

CHAPTER XIII.

CHAPTER XIV.

CHAPTER XV.

CHAPTER XVI.

CHAPTER XX.

CHAPTER XXI.

CHAPTER XXII.

CHAPTER XXIII.

A COUNTRY CURATE'S AUTOBIOGRAPHY.

CHAPTER I.

As with new wine intoxicated both,
They swim in mirth, and fancy that they feel
Divinity within them, breeding wings
Wherewith to scorn the earth.   MILTON.

IT is, no doubt, a trite remark that, if our modern travellers would first of all make themselves acquainted with the scenery and manners of home, much good English money would be saved from continental dissipation ; and, what is far more desirable, in a social as well as political view, many good English subjects would settle down, in a healthy and well-affected state of mind, in the bosom of their own country,—

be it the sea-girt Britain or her emerald consort of the
main. *The monkey that had seen the world* may,
honestly and good-naturedly, be held forth as a pattern to be avoided by all well-disposed citizens ; and,
surely, no proficiency is really less enviable than that
in virtue of which a man claims his acquaintance in
voluptuous Italy or restless France—among Scythians
or Barbarians ; but has no knowledge of his native
hills, and few endearments of a compatriot and truly
congenial character.

With such ideas as these, the writer of this little
book calls to mind a season in which, free as the
winds, light as the clouds, and willing as the streams
which play around her mountains, he wandered in
the Western Highlands of Scotland ; and here, early
as it may be to apostrophize, he turns aside to place
on record the generous effect now produced—now,
that nought but

> " Fond Memory brings the light
> Of other days around me."

Gentle, courteous reader, there is a time of life in
which the blood is warm. Circling gaily in its channels, few impediments interrupt its course. It is an
interregnum between the despotic rule of school-
masters, tutors, proctors and moderators, and the
dynasty of care. Prize it highly, if thou have it

now; for, with a mind not more sordid, not fallen lower than the primæval cause and curse have rendered unavoidable, it is a time of golden dreams—it is a time in which love, friendship, and honour are thy graces. If it be in store for thee, bear with becoming patience the restraints, as, one by one, they loose their hold, which parents and guardians seasonably impose; and remember always, that our friend—once too familiar, now too long forgotten—counsels well, with regard to the " *quicquid corrigere est nefas,*" which may now be fastened on thee—" *Levius fit patientiâ.*"

But if, with me, you stand on tiptoe, and through the medley of events, endeavour to look back upon those sunny scenes which once acknowledged our individual presence, why, let us not repine. Let us learn to acknowledge that, though morning suns were bright and alluring, noon, ay, afternoon and evening too, have charms. Under the heat and labour of the day, domestic objects fling over us a grateful shade; nor are the chills and damps of evening less cheeringly warded off by those rational joys which crown the later scenes of life.

To begin is easy, in almost all things but writing. Perhaps it may be an omen in my favour, that we smoothly glide into vicious courses; and the very difficulty with which we enter on the rugged path of

virtue (happy thought!) may account for the labouring effort which brings to the birth this Autobiography. It is, however, now done. *He gives twice
who gives quickly ;* and, once for all, I give myself to
public indulgence, while I trace the simple annals of
a few years' progress in this interesting world.

———

B—— was one of those fortunate men who, after
having pleasantly passed the season of undergradu-
ateship, find themselves dignified with the immortal
honour of a place among wranglers, and gently
sliding into the importance of a fellowship. I was
one of those non-fortunate men, who scramble to
shore from the wreck of college-life, and think themselves happy—"*post tot naufragia*"— in having lost
every thing but themselves. But, though thus dis-
similar in academic posture, there was a great con-
geniality and sympathy between us. We had both a
rational tinge of romance. We were both in love
with nature, and liked her the more, the more extra-
vagant and domineering she appeared. We regarded
the artificial parts of life as only so many vessels, in
which were served the rich and savoury viands of
sentiment and intellectuality.

Thus disposed, we sat at breakfast one summer's
morning, not a dozen years ago, in the small parlour
of an inn on the western shore of Loch Lomond.

"How strange," said he, "that we should have reached this house in safety, undrowned and un-plundered, from the opposite shore! Why, that fellow's mountain dew was smooth as honey, but ran deep as Acheron. Surely, the enchantress of that cavern must have robbed us of our wits for spite!"

"Nay, it was in the way of nature. 'Twas no landsman's task to row obliquely across that lake; and then, the offspring of the illicit still stole too easily upon our worn-out energies. In truth, we were not criminally—"

"Oh, no—only in the last stage—*sans everything*. It was the mere effect of drinking fire instead of water; of being in the bowels of the earth instead of on her bosom; and of toasting, with that honest Scotch scoundrel, the memory of Rob Roy, Burns, and Sir Walter, instead of paying due attention to our own."

"But, I say, B——, how did we ever get down the headlong face of that rock, which we climbed with so much difficulty by the light of the moon, into our boat again? I have some recollection of being carried by our guide."

"My memory serves me just thus far. You pro-posed, with more gallantry than prudence, *a health to all the bonnie lassies of Caledonia*. Our companion, touched with patriotic fire, quickly filled again, gave *the honour of England, and all her sons and daughters,* tippled his glass, and then, taking his lamp in one hand, and yourself under the other arm, bade me follow. The same broken, winding passage brought us back again to the light of heaven; and then, after having cautioned me to remain where I was, he carefully descended with you to the boat. Having re-ascended, with all the agility of a mountain cat, he helped me down, just as some son of Neptune gallants a faultering maiden from the deck of a man-of-war to the tiny boat by her side; and, with strict injunctions, (observing that the rock was *mony a fothom* more below than above the surface of the loch) left me to the care of you, while he returned to the cavern for the things which, in his concern for us, he had left behind. I can just collect some remembrance of a cold shudder, as he jumped into the middle of the boat, some half-stifled apprehensions as he opened a prodigious clasp-knife, cut away the mooring, and, stoutly grasping both the oars, pulled away like one bent on desperate purposes."

"Thank Heaven! we are here."

"And so is he, too. He waits in the house, declaring that he will have nothing (save whiskey), but is determined to drink our health before he leaves us."

"Honest fellow! there was *that* about the man, I

could have placed a hundred lives in his hand, and yet we seem to have escaped the jaws of destruction in having got free of him."

"Well, let us have him in, shall we?"

So saying, B—— touched the bell, and a few seconds and a few minutes brought him before us, and made us acquainted with all that which may be surmised from the dialogue above—how, like impassioned rivals, we sang sonnets to the moon, and how his oars kept time with our alternate modulations—how, at other times, we sang together, and he joined in chorus, the scraps of Scotch melodies which we managed to remember—how, in short, occurred every incident of a night to which, however ill-suited to the gravity of my present calling, I cannot look back but with a sensation of something very like delight.

The audience of our mysterious friend—for mysterious he was—gifted with an elegance of sentiment and strength of language which contrasted strangely with the dress of an inland sailor, or, as he appeared in another light, patron of a nest of smuggling distillers—was suddenly broken off by the arrival of the post, bringing for each of us that always welcome, though often disagreeable, minister of suspense—a *letter*.

CHAPTER II.

A man is an ill husband of his honour, that entereth
into any action, the failing wherein may disgrace him
more than the carrying of it through can honour him.

BACON.

My father, a professional man of ——shire, had sent
me to college, under strong impressions of parental
fondness and partiality; and, as I was *not* considered " the fool of the family"—for, indeed, we were a
very bright set,—had marked out for me—dear, sanguine
man—nearly the highest honours of the University;
and, now that I had disappointed all those anticipations,—not, in that I had, instead of honour, earned
disgrace; but, because a simple and unassuming post
in the middle of the *poll*—that *summum desiderium* of
so many—was wormwood to the hopes of misplaced
ambition—I was unhappy, inasmuch as I was in-
nocently a source of some unhappiness to him. I had
achieved that consummation which is the subject of

rejoicing to most; but, because in achieving it I had suffered more lofty laurels to be carried out of reach, I seemed to have been accessory to a parent's disappointment—I seemed to be guilty, I was miserable—in the phrase of the day, I had *done nothing*, and had thereby undone every thing.

I had, however, every hope that some little conversation would remove all the ill-grounded chagrin of my father; and, as I reasoned with myself so successfully, was not without assurance that he too would see the entire fallacy of that *rule nisi* which is derived from the " Cambridge Bachelors' Commencement."

The letter which I had just received determined me in my resolution to seek personally that reconciliation, the want of which had placed me for some months at a distance from the parental roof—in the enjoyment (if, under such a want it were enjoyment) of my friend B.'s society: for he, *pupilizing* during the long vacation at the little county-town of Inverary, had invited me to become his companion. But, as the subject of my defence, which had often occupied my serious attention, was now, more earnestly than ever, canvassed in my mind, it may be allowed to form a legitimate part of this Biography; and the reader will perhaps pardon the introduction of *thoughts,* the validity of which has been amply tested by the circumstances of my subsequent course of life.

There are two methods, all the world knows, of obtaining the degree of B.A. at Cambridge—the one, by *taking an honour* in mathematics; the other, by passing through the ordeal of a general examination. The means of accomplishing either are well defined and known beforehand. There are *men* in the University who can *cram* the aspirant, provided that he have the base of a common understanding and will *read*, to any degree of plumpness. So that, though a candidate may be somewhat higher or lower than he expected, (according to the turn of the *moderation,** if he be a mathematical scholar—according to the chances of the *examination,** if a general scholar) he has no one but himself to blame, if he fail of obtaining the object in view. It is a race in which all who run may obtain the *quantum suff.*—a lottery in which there are no actual blanks. It comes, however, by comparison, to be considered otherwise. *Comparison* is a good word. There are *three degrees*—the *Wrangler's,* which is, *superlatively,*—the *Senior-Optime's,* which is, *comparatively,*—and the *Junior Optime's,* which is, *positively,* more honourable than the degree obtained by him who has undergone the general exa-

* The judges of the one class are called *Moderators;* of the other, *Examiners.*

mination. But why, I must say I have never yet been able to see a sufficient cause.

The *honour-man* gains his degree by mathematics only—in other words, by a scholastic course of reading, and cramming into his memory a variety of Definitions, Solutions of Problems, Theorems, Scholia, &c. (commonly called *Book-work*)—the results of the labours of different philosophers down from Newton to the last *petit-maitre* whose " treatise" is before the world.

The *poll-man** gains his degree by a scanty display of general information in Classics, in moral and argumentative Theology, such as Paley exhibits it, in a shadow of Logic, according to Locke, and in the lower branches of the Mathematics.

Each, according to his proficiency, occupies a place in his respective department;—i. e. down from the *Senior Wrangler* to the lowest *Junior Op.* on the one hand, and down from the *captain* to the last man of the honourless band.

But, it should be observed that, as between these two there is a great *gulf* fixed which receives the refuse of the former, so at the end of the latter there is a *falling-off* of some. Those go away without *an honour*, but with *a degree*—these, with nothing, but

---

* One of ὅι πολλοι, or *the many.*

without a feather, are significantly said to be *plucked:*
—those the friendly *gulf* sustains, these stripped of
their supporting plumes sink, to rise again only at the
bar of some more auspicious (commonly a private bye-
term) examination.*

Let it, then, be fairly weighed, whether, in point of
real merit, the *poll-man* should not be rather accounted *honourable*—" A fellow-feeling makes one
wondrous kind." He *must* have some general information—he must be able to read Homer and Virgil,
to write something like his own language, and to
say his Multiplication-table; whereas, the *honour-
man* may, like a horse in a mill, be confined to his
own narrow sphere, with a head capable of retaining
a good deal of that which, by constant repetition, has
been worked into it.   Like Master (what's his
name?) who can, in a moment, tell you how many
inches of whipcord would encircle the planet Mercury,
but cannot tell why Mercury is called a planet, or

---

* There are other *technicalities* connected with this ordeal,
which, however, come under the denomination of *slang*. The
last Wrangler, the last Senior Op. and the last Junior Op. are,
respectively, yclep'd—" The golden spoon," " The silver spoon,"
and " The wooden spoon ;" and by a metonymy, the *men,* who
get these places, may be said to have got these articles.   The last
twelve of the *poll.* have been (indecorously) called " *Apostles ;*"
and those who are infra-ordinary, being classed alphabetically, I
have heard named " Elegant Extracts."

why the planet is called Mercury, Mr. Senior Wrangler (and this is taking the extremest case) *may* be able to work out, by memory, vast problems of scientific research which mighty men have solved before, even as the cur may yelp at the heels of the fleetest courser, but cannot, perhaps, give one ray of information to the admiring multitude who applaud his wisdom; and such men are the *fuimus Troës* of the *Cambridge Philosophical Society.**

There is a " previous examination," in justice be it said, (instituted of late years) by which all students are supposed to be laid under an obligation to display some classical knowledge. But, what is it? a short Greek, and a short Latin subject, most literally done into vile English by the press, and one of the Gospels or the Acts. A whole year is given in which to prepare for this august tribunal; and he must be obtuse indeed who cannot be even *parrotized* so as to meet its terrors. Such, however, are these terrors that, to escape a second and enlarged edition of

---

* In making this observation, it is not by any means insinuated (for such an insinuation would be base as groundless) that there are a great many wranglers who are thus confined to their single glory; but there are some, and the writer has known one Senior Wrangler who, by length of time and dint of labour bestowed on a single branch of knowledge—and what cannot be done by these means?—earned a *literary* fame to which he was any thing but entitled.

them, they frighten into mathematics many a *Cantab* who would be glad of a dispensation from the honour of being immortalized in the *Cambridge University Calendar.*

But, if the evil terminated in Trumpington Street, or on Castle-hill even, there would be no room for remarks which doubtless appear invidious. As Academic exercises, mathematics have every merit; but, as the qualification for all the preferments of after-life, they are plainly inadmissible to calm and un-biassed judgment. If a man be a better teacher, a more polished advocate, a more zealous clergyman, or a more effective preacher, a sounder statesman, judge or magistrate, because his name is attached to one of the legs of the *Tripos,** the Pythia herself, methinks, could not divine the *reason why.* Content even to let these *distingués* nestle themselves into all the pretty pickings of their respective colleges—let them be V.-Cs, heads-of-houses, fellows, tutors, proctors, taxors, college-deans, librarians, bursars—they worked for it, they have earned it, and they have it. But, I say, let not the free and healthy circulation of public life be checked and benumbed by such a fallacy—let not the working curate starve in a discharge of duties by which the goodwill and approbation of a parish are

* The *three* classes of Wranglers, Senior Optimes and Junior Optimes, are understood in this word.

derived to him, while a man, it may be of far inferior talents, walks into beneficial fatness, merely and solely because he was a Wrangler. *Fuimus Troës* should not (and old Æneas himself must admit it) be the motto which gains men the power and choice of *settlement,* because it insures success, wherever they prefer to fix their residence; though it may be a suitable passport to the presence of Minerva, as she sits on high amid the Cambridge Philosophical Society. I hold it monstrous that a man, who once knew all Euclid by rote, and has entirely forgotten both the integral and differential calculus, should be deemed preferable to him who, having laid his foundation in general literature, has built up a superstructure from every loop-hole of which the beams of useful knowledge may direct and inform his fellow-creatures, and, rendering them happy, lead them on to the noblest contemplations of which the human mind is capable.

But, I suppose it ever will be so: and, therefore, come Poverty, but bring Contentment with thee, and I will learn to live in the light of my own conscience, to leave the monopolists of human favour (in this as in all other things) to glad themselves, like the glow-worm, in the illumination of their own fancied superiority, and to derive the intellectual food of my existence from the far more expansive excellences of an universe. The world is gulled by Fame, and she, returning to her place among the inhabitants of a nobler sphere, laughs at the victims of her caprice: so, when we retire to the closet of our own feelings, may we experience the satisfaction of knowing ourselves superior, though, mayhap, no one else can find it out.

Under such comfortable and accommodating notions, I penned a hasty reply to my anxious father, and set my things in order for a journey to Edinburgh, whence I purposed without delay to start for home— that haven of endearments which reconcile even the wretch to his lot, and without which the most prosperous voyager in life is wretch indeed.

CHAPTER III.

" I stood in * *, on the bridge of sighs."

BYRON.

IT is but a small part of my plan to detail the circumstances of outward imagery. I rather deal with a biography of thoughts. Else, the reader might be gratified with the picture of a steamer on the magnificent Loch Lomond, studded with its beautiful miniatures of islands; and of the various characters which swell the list of tourists. I might dole out the *tædia* of a passage in the track-boat along " the Great Union Canal," through tunnels and over aqueducts of various extent and of considerable interest or beauty; and would dwell upon the enchanting view of Linlithgow by moonlight, with the silvery lake behind the castle, and the light from the Carron iron-works, flaring in the midnight sky;—thus bringing my reader, *paulatim*, to the Athenian pretensions of

Auld Reeky; but others have done all this, and I did
it in a Diary which is long since consigned to the
place of all lost—*Mi Lector*, be pleased to walk with
me round the corner which, in that day, it was necessary to double, before, in coming from the General
Post-office, you could gain a station on the High-
bridge in Edinburgh.

Upon this bridge I stood, looking down upon the
stream of population below. It is a bridge across a
valley, in fact, across a broad and irregular street;
and to indulge in this speculation is, like the gaze at
St. Dunstan's *quondam* clubmen, a mark or sign of
recent importation to the Athens of the Scots.
Quickly turning round at the sound of a voice, which
seemed even more than familiar to one who thought
himself nearly sequestered from all men he had ever
seen before, I perceived, in earnest conversation as
they shot, like a vision, by me, two of Scotland's
fairest daughters. One, the fairer and taller, was
known to me, intimately, if I may borrow a word
from my feelings; but, perhaps, would not have
known me at all, had I claimed acquaintance.

If any one, who reads these pages, have ever felt
himself so hopelessly alone in the world that he
would gladly hold a conversation with the eyes of his
dog—that feeling which is apt to steal over one,
alone and unknown in a strange city, where so many

happy and so many wretched faces disown all sympathy with an alien, and yet where so much passing good-humour and politeness only paint more vividly the chasm between hearts which own no common attraction—he may surmise that with glistening eyes I followed the direction which the females took, until my steps, instinctively, were in the path which they had left behind them.

From the foot of the bridge, at which I had ascended it, they turned to the left, and pursued their course and conversation, both alike rapid and heedless of all observation, along Prince's Street—that lovely lounge—how unlike the Prince's Street of London!—until they arrived at a door, nearly opposite the Episcopal chapel, which received them at once without knocking.

"Well, it is a shame," thought I, as I retraced my steps, "that I, so soon to be admitted to a sacred office, should dally at the heels of a highland girl who would not even know me, perhaps, and for whom I can have no real affection—a mere creature of the imagination, attired in the most shadowy reality—whom I never saw but once, and hardly ever spoke to."

I had lost the mail—the only coach by which I could reach my father's house on the day appointed. I had also thrown away the money advanced for my

place; and should inevitably incur the expense of
another day's delay in Edinburgh. These, in spite
of all the enthusiasm which had scarcely yet relaxed
its hold upon me, and which in vain I endeavoured to
reason down, were reflections which produced no
small mortification, and had the effect of rendering
my countenance (as repeated bumps and collisions
bare testimony) much more downcast, and my pace
much more tardy, than when I careered it in the opposite direction.

But, the blast of bugles from the castle gave a
fresh channel to my meditations; and the tattoo of
drums and trumpets which succeeded, flinging its
martial and admonitory notes across the valley between, and re-echoing from side to side, or, at other
times, cooped up within the castle-walls, giving that
oft-reverberated sound which fires the imagination
with thoughts of ancient chivalry, had the effect of
not only reconciling me to my losses, but winning
me to the notion that I was happy in having another
day to stay in a city which possessed so many and
such varied attractions.

Musing thus, in happier mood, I found myself at
the entrance of my tavern; and here I soon gave
way, in all the composure and elasticity of a summer's evening, to a regular, methodical, but romantic,
reverie—inviting and entertaining just such ideas as

were perfectly agreeable, and rejecting at once the overtures of the more objectionable—a happy condition, it is true, for a lover; but not so serviceable to a young divine.

Nothing could be more reasonable than that one, intended, as I was, for holy orders, should be sincere and disinterested, consulting real and honourable feeling, not sordid views of gain or advancement. Nay—it was the path of *duty;* and he, who was to preach to others the worthlessness of all earthly treasures, ought, by his own example, to give vigour to his doctrine. She was not what the world calls great; and the love, therefore, was not the staring Cupid that presides over, or concocts, *good matches:* but the heart was the touchstone of all that was really good, and great, and desirable, and conduct, in obedience to its dictates, must not only, at length, gain the applause of good men, but have, for its warrant and support, the countenance of Heaven.

During the rumination, of which this is a mere epitome, it never entered my mind that I might be pursuing a phantom, which had indeed twice appeared, but might perchance never walk again; or, that, with all my vaunted sincerity and disinterestedness, I might be the most self-determined admirer that ever followed in the rosy train of blind-fold love. It never occurred to me that, discarding, as I professed to do, all worldly motives, I might be most covetous of a treasure to which, not merely had my own feelings attached an inordinate value, but another might have a paramount and affianced claim.

But, no drawbacks operated upon the course of my cogitations—"All went merry as a marriage-bell"—and, borrowing a glow of sentiment from the warm lustre of sunset, I strolled up the Calton Hill, contemplated Nelson's monument, and felt all-sufficient in myself to brave the storms of a world in arms against an act so improvident as the perpetration of marriage (if it should come to this) without, what the lawyers call, *consideration.* Lord Bacon has written—"A numerous married clergy, giving life to great numbers of idlers, or persons never to work, is very dangerous to a state, by creating mouths without creating a suitable portion of labour at the same time;" but, in spite of all remonstrances, and, without staying to inquire why (if they do not) the children of clergymen should not work, I was fully possessed with a conclusion that all clergymen ought to be at full liberty to marry; I placed, in opposition to Bacon's exceptionable remark, what I found in Atterbury—that a married clergy, " by teaching their flocks how to carry themselves in their relations of husbands and wives, parents and children,

have without question adorned the gospel, glorified
God, and benefited man, much more than they
could have done in the devoutest and strictest celibacy;" and, having already made two or three unsuc-
cessful offers to enter the porch of Hymen with the
regular and approved formalities, felt that I gratified
a pique in resolving to climb into the temple by
some way unknown to the vulgar, while I obeyed
that imagined law of necessity—for the expediency of
a married clergy soon towers up into necessity—to
which I was so soon intended to be amenable.   Thus,
how well I represented the species—ever ready to
make sure of what their own wayward appetites long
for, but diffident of themselves when the object is
proposed according to rule.

But I was impelled, or, rather, fortified, in the prosecution of my lucreless ambition by such ideas—
whether well, or ill, or not at all, grounded, my
reader will determine—as these.   The ministry of the
church, thought I, must be either a worldly or a
spiritual occupation—I had no inclination to view it
as that divino-secular employment which, after all, it
perhaps is.   If worldly, the hire of the labourer
ought to be adequate to his wants, these wants
being, in a Protestant church, to be extended to the
possibility of matrimony and its contingencies; specially, when this church has, in her own coffers, the

means of thus supplying the lawful wants of her ministers. If spiritual, then, as I concluded, the ways
and means should be a question not permitted to dis-
tract the mind and relax the sacred efforts of the
divine. To what extent the expenses of a clergyman's
family should be carried, the laws of society seem to
have decreed : he is thereby required to appear in a
decent state of comfortable superiority to the wants
and emergencies of life; and few sincere clergymen
have any desire to overstep the limits which are thus
indulgently prescribed.

It may be questioned, whether the influx of men of
fortune to the ministerial office be an acquisition to be
valued, or an ornament to be dispensed with; and the
best evidence may, perhaps, be derived from a consideration of the comparative efficiency of the two
grades (if I may so speak) of clergymen.

The poor, to whom the gospel is specially preached,
are decidedly won by that faithful exercise of duty
which a mere competency is so well calculated to promote; and the middle classes follow as surely in the
same path, if we may not add most of the upper ranks,
so far as these are accessible to the influence of the
pastoral office: but, once let the clergyman be known
to be actually poor—in plain terms, unable to answer
the demands upon him for expenses, next to unavoidable if he have a family, and gratuities equally in-

dispensable if he be the curate of a parish ——; and the certain consequence is, that he meets with such altered demeanour in those who formerly paid him some marks of respect, encounters such efforts of scandal, has such intimations from his creditors in the shape of certain repeated accounts of *bills delivered*, and experiences so many proofs (indescribable and, to the layman, unimaginable,) of declining usefulness, that he must be a man of apostolic energy indeed, if he do not yield to the blast, and imbibe a portion of disgust with the bitter draughts he is compelled to swallow.

On the other hand, the man of fortune, to whose influence the clerical distinction is, perhaps, but the least important appendage, having the means, and generally the disposition, to mix with the highest circles, is too apt to consign the endearing office of curate to a minister of the other grade, and to become, in the eyes of at least the vulgar, and prejudiced, (and these are, perhaps, the most numerous, as they require the most anxious attention, in the whole flock), a being out of the reach of ordinary men, and identified only with the distinguished few.

I dreamed, indeed, in this state of embryo, of the apostolical communion of goods: and, when the cavil arose in my mind, relative to the *motion*, and *call*, of the *Holy Spirit*, (in the former of which the *deacon* has declared his trust, and in the latter the *priest* his conviction) knowing that God worketh as he will without respect of rich or poor, I concluded that those of the clergy, who were men of fortune, (to use my former designation,) might reasonably be required, either not to draw from the *common* fund of Church property, or to distribute, after due attention to the claims of kindred, their *goods* to feed the poor—but, alas! what had I to do with it? Time enough, when I should be one of those whose plighted vows had gained them entrance to the sacred order; and, in the playfulness of one who was yet a *layman*, I ventured to indite a note, so dissonant (and yet, I know not whether a less fastidious ear would not discover some strains of harmony, were the *coda* allowed to be added; though according to the *spirit of the age*, it was so dissonant) from the precocious tone in which I had just discussed some of the proprieties of the clerical character, that I cannot even append it to this chapter.

CHAPTER IV.

The circling hills, all black and wild,
Are o'er its slumbers darkly piled,
———- ——— where fár below,
The everlasting waters flow,
And, round the precipices vast,
Dance to the music of the blast.

MALCOLM'S *Poems.*

SCARCELY had the life of another day begun, when I penned the following effusion to her, for whose sake, or, at least, on whose account, I again opened my eyes in the " land of the mountain and the flood,"— the production of last evening, being deemed too ethereal for the ken of mortal eye, sobered into vision by the surrounding objects of a busy world :—

" Miss C——ll,

" (For the heart, which now endeavours to address you, disdains every expression of words by which love and admiration are wont to be conveyed). Permit me, by way of introduction, to remind you of the moment in which I first beheld you.—That moment was consecrated by a love as warm as the circumstances of its birth were sudden and extraordinary; and it is in this hour of calm reflection, that I seek to avow to you its continued existence.

"You will remember the appearance of two strangers at your father's door, one evening—a fortnight ago tomorrow. Do you remember the one who lingered behind, and, as you stood waiting by that jutting rock to which you had conducted them, (like the guardian angel of their route,) to see that your instructions were observed, waved a hand to signify assurance of the way? He it is who now ventures to lay at your feet, at once, this declaration of an indomitable love and an offer of his heart and affections upon terms which you yourself (should you deign—and oh! you will not refuse?—to accept them,) are besought to impose.

" By the providence of an indulgent Disposer of events, I stood on the High-bridge, last evening, as you passed with (do I conjecture wrongly?) your sister. I followed you to the house at which I leave this—I learned that it was your residence; and I now wait, at the door of the Episcopal Chapel, to receive one word of encouragement, or to be consigned to hopelessness for ever. Be kind, as you are beautiful; and, as you resemble those happy beings whose occupation is holy joy, be merciful to

" Your devoted,

*——— *————.' "

Such was the act and deed—such the condition of the autobiographer.

" Poor Romeo is already dead !
Stabb'd with a white wench's black eye,
Run through the ear with a love-song."

My reader is, perhaps, anxious to know the particulars of that *first-sight* to which I alluded in my note; and, as it may be conceived to have borne portentously upon my after-life, a sketch of them, with an account of the expedition which led to them, is here offered to his notice.

On the same side of Loch Lomond as the cave of Rob Roy, to which allusion was made in the first chapter but some few miles farther down in the direction of Balloch Ferry, there is a place called Rowerdennam Inn. It is at or near the foot of Ben-Lomond, or, to speak in a more appropriate figure, it is placed, like the beazel of a ring, upon one of his extended toes. From this Inn, B—— and myself, having furnished ourselves with what they call a *guide*, and him with a *lomb-leg* and its appurtenances of bread, salt, and whiskey, set out, in the early afternoon of one of the pleasant days we passed together in that delightful and eventful neighbourhood, with a determination of purpose to the summit of the mountain. The day was much more favourable to the ascending, than the many hot ones which had preceded it; and, as we breasted the rugged side of this, the Caledonian Ande, we had little reason to complain of fatigue. A little rivalry in the display of agility and perseverance, however, brought on, at last, that singularly oppressive sensation of weariness in the thighs, which they, who have toiled to the ball of St. Paul's, will not need to have explained: and, as B— strided away, over rock and hether, I more than once called a halt, while I lay to regale my limbs, and to feast my eyes with the beauty of the lake, as we rose above it, studded with its many and picturesque islands. It was the marble pavement, whereon the giant, which is nature's husband, had cast the verdant chaplet, scattered into fragments, from his brows, before he reposed in sullen but majestic grandeur upon his mountain-couch.

We had performed perhaps five of the six or seven miles of variously inclined plane, when we both turned round to behold, in admiration, a dense and dark cloud which, like a veil of "sackcloth of hair," was rapidly overspreading the scene behind us. The hues of different objects were lost in the gradations of shade which now enveloped them all; the islands being discernible only by their deeper gloom, while the mountains around us were blending fast with the general darkness.

Half bewailing the loss of prospect from the summit, and half rejoicing in the anticipation of a coming summer-storm, we quickened our pace, and soon gained the point on which (a mere rod to the eye below) a vast trunk of a tree has been reared, as the staff of an ensign, or as a beacon to the wild mountaineers of Charley's days, or the black-mail worthies of a less amiable generation. There was, in the rude strength of this object, a something which, placed as it and we were, brought forcibly to mind the events of Bannockburn and Preston-pans, the ponderous morglay of the Scottish chieftain, (as you see it in Dumbarton Castle,) the rent-paying claymore, and all the recollections of even ruder ages, when savage murders went unpunished, and horrors were perpetrated, such as Macduff took vengeance for, under the cloak of the brutal spirit of clanship.

We soon found that we were not sole monarchs of the summit; for a band of tourists were grouped behind the compressed and cowering peak of the mountain, giving that satisfaction to their mouths which the clouds denied to their eyes. All was indistinct; around, above, and below, the quality of the prospect was *fog;* and the party we had come in sight of looked more of optical illusions than proper men : and while the rain, mingled with hail, fell, or rather was discharged, upon us, with a fury which rendered recklessness the height of wisdom, we followed their example, and beckoned to our attendant to approach with his welcome store.

Well acquainted with the localities of the mountain, he quickly fetched water from the nearest spring, and full soon, with the help of our guide and of the like functionary of our friends from Glasgow or Paisley, (as, with an unchristian sneer, we surmised,) both meat and drink were discussed, and old Hugo in possession of the bone.

We had, consequently, leisure to enjoy the sublimities of the storm, now increased by thunders louder than the inhabitants of a champaign ever hear, and by lightnings which, darting from the exploding clouds around and below us, seemed to rush with mad delight to the lower regions of the plain. It was novel, it was grand, and it was alarming to us, to hear the unutterable crash (as it were of a finished world, but in truth,) of cloud with cloud, and to look *down upon* the sources of lightning, while we stood exalted higher than the conflicting elements ; and as the demons of the storm seemed at times to hurl their thunders at the head of Ben Lomond, it was horribly bewitching to be amidst the lightnings, with rattling peals about our elbows, and we looked at each other's paleness with all the interesting solemnity which may be supposed to have characterized the " thane of Glamis" and his comrade, in their interview with the *choppy-fingered* damsels.

Being most handsomely drenched,—the black dye from B——'s travelling cap running in streams down his cheeks, and the green from my gambroon jacket variegating in like manner my " whitey-brown" trowsers,—we had fully enjoyed the more bustling part of the scene, and would have gladly said, " *Hold! enough!* " when the conical heads of the surrounding hills began to be dimly visible, and the islands on the loch again peeped through their veil. He who has been here will remember that there is an assemblage of mountain-tops, about the head of Loch Long, west of Ben Lomond, among which *the Cobler* and his *wife* take a conspicuous station; and to him I need not endeavour to describe the majestic character which the whole assumes. To us they were indescribably grand. As the storm cleared off, this bold and irregular zigzag line of peaks and headlands was thrown out in fine relief by the red and lurid light which, based (so to speak) in the horizon, shone

with a dull but fiery splendour from behind them.
They seemed as the bulwarks of a place of torment—
the ramparts of a prison-house of suffering souls!
and if ever papist really thought of purgatory, he
might have fancied it behind those mountains.

Fully satisfied with the result of our enterprise, so
far as it had gone, we now dismissed our guide, notwithstanding his expostulations and warnings, and
prepared to descend by another side of the mountain.
He pointed out to us a stream (at that moment lying,
like a silver serpent, smiling in the sun) which would
lead us, if we adhered to its course, in our progress
to the place marked out for our night's retreat; and
we descended gaily, with the one in view and the
other in anxious anticipation; for though the *animal*,
as well as *mental*, had been well sustained, yet the
effects of the pelting we had endured, together with
that sort of stupefaction which fairly puts an end to
all former *regimes*, were such as to call loudly for
reinforcements in behalf of the former.

We were supporting each other's spirits, by mutual
congratulations on the scenery we had witnessed, when
both at once—*fortemque Gyan, fortemque Cloanthum*
—we lost sight of the stream which had, till just now,
glittered along the plain below. Clouds intervening,
we were exposed to, and fell into the error of winding, for want of an object, round the side of the

mountain; and the *halloa!* of our abandoned guide, into whose track our spiral propensity had brought us, but whom, in our elastic boundings down the declivities, we had far outstripped, reduced us to an acknowledgment of our folly. Being put right again, as far as we could be in a Scotch mist, we, however, persisted in our determination to adventure, not only rejecting the proffered gratuity of his guidance, but turning a deaf ear to a tale of a *jontleman* who was lost and starved to death in the same parts but a year before, and took an affectionate and grateful leave of our humble Mentor. Feeling sure that we must soon reach the stream, the sight of which the envious clouds denied us, we dashed on as buoyantly as before, tumbling at one time over craggy impediments, at another plunging into hether, drenched as we were, up to the middle.

Strong coveys of grouse, and, now and then, the noble black-cock, took wing at our approach; the traces of man's handiwork, too, were observed in the sheep-hovels which we met with, but no welcome chimney smoking gave sign of his proximity. We had now descended to the plain, a conviction which was brought forcibly home to us by the increased labour of walking under a burthen of wet clothes. The time, in which we ought to have reached the rivulet, was more than spent, and yet we saw nothing

of it. Cold, wet, and weary, we now reproached
ourselves (each himself out of courtesy), with head-
strong foolishness. We would have kindled a fire of
some of the turf which we found under sheds, but,
alas! the *lucifers* were spoiled with the rain. Food
we had none—silver and gold we had both; but,
fine moral reflection! not all the wealth of Crœsus
could have now procured for us a single bannock;
and, as we gravely worked out the conclusion, not all
that we possessed could purchase a *muchkin* of " the
real mountain dew." What was to be done? We
had more than once been led into a temptation to
" *go-about;*" and, though we had endeavoured to
observe a strict correspondence between all our respective turnings and returnings, still we must have
lost in the long-run, and were too evidently far out
of our proper course. The sun *would have* guided us;
but all was fog and rain, clouds and doubts and
misgivings. We had been directed to cross the
stream, at a well-described bridge; and, coming at
last to the edge of a ravine, in the bottom of which
water was indeed abundant, we concluded this was
the course of the long-lost current, that we had left
the bridge far away, and that now we must cross, as
best we might.

Into this pass, then,—neither more nor less than
the celebrated pass of Aberfoil,—with a difficulty

which, though great in retrospect, was hardly felt at the time, we descended; and, after running up and down in search of the best apparent ford, we dashed into the stream, which was in many parts a frightful torrent, as heedless of the water as wet skins and empty stomachs may be supposed to have rendered us. After indescribable fatigue we reached the summit of the opposite cliff; and, here sitting down—seriously moved by the questionableness of the manner in which we should pass the night now nearly upon us—we looked back upon the flood through which we had just waded, and then before us upon a dreary heath confined within the limits of a fog, and appealing to the senses only by the pitter-pattering of the rain. Thousands of better men undergo as much fatigue and infinitely more privation commonly; but to us the trial had been, and continued to be, severe and appalling. Cold and hunger, and exhaustion of strength, heightened by disappointment, which almost amounted to despair, had taken full possession of us ; and I verily believe that, after a walk of three or four more miles, one more blow would have laid us up, or down, for the night, when an object too cheering for description was, by degrees, confirmed to our inquiring eyes. A row of Highland cottages was certainly revealed by that line of chimney-like elevations which were dimly shadowed through the atmosphere, just now relaxing into a smile of daylight ; and, with ecstatic hope, we *ran* towards the object, as if anticipating the but too evident design of the returning fog to snatch it from our view. At last, the *oh ! quando te aspiciam !* was lost in an exultation of joy, when we clearly descried the whiter wreath of smoke, and hurried down, our sorrows all forgotten, to the goal of deliverance.

Guess at our appearance—our light summer-dresses blended in one general aspect of watery wretchedness—my straw hat hanging about my head, and poor B——'s cap even yielding its precise and formal qualities to the circumstances of the time—never was such a pitilessly pelted pair of tourists. Approaching the door of what seemed to be the principal one of the tenements (for, it had a rapper, and other indications of superiority), no wary dun, with ear inclined and stooping form, ever knocked with more judicious modesty than did friend B——. Had it been in the sunny morning, some familiarising voice would have summoned, through the opened door, the attendance of an inmate. Now, in the evening of adversity, and within the gripe of real affliction, we sought, as for an alms, that for which we were prepared to astonish the simple swain with our liberality. Such is the influence, perhaps, of the atmosphere upon animal spirits, and, through these, upon animal deportment. Such may be an example and a proof of that rule of distinction between the manners of different nations—that, while the Englishman's backward, hesitating, and somewhat confused entrance to a dining-room would be looked for in one whose intention it was to purloin the forks and spoons; the inhabitant of more sunny shores—our neighbour from *la belle France*, for instance—displays a brazen, staring impudence (in the eyes of J. B.), which would seem to set down all the rest of the company for a *corps dramatique* of puppets, over which he reigns as showman. But, without further ethicizing, B——'s fingers were *not* upon the latch—his rap was double, but simple—not the tap of a mendicant, nor the *rat-tat-tan* of a man *out of the common;* but something *in medio,* and, therefore, *safest.* The low growl of the house-dog, and that *concord of sweet sounds*—the harmony of domestic, female voices—sufficiently proved to us that suffering had now triumphed; and we were already giving our wet and muddy extremities an instinctive shaking, when the sticking door (seldom used but when the rent-day came), opened with a jerk, and revealed to our astonished eyes—not one of those mountain hags, with pipe short and black on one side of the mouth, and a little cloud on the other, whom we sometimes met with—not a brawny Highlander, backed by his beautiful, sleek, black sheep-dog—no ; nor a stout young Scotch lassie, with bare feet and ankles, and a carter's whip in her hand—but a paragon of beauty, symmetry, and elegance—a nymph, the nymph which adorned and sanctified these wilds of nature—a sylph, whose duty seemed to be to live in contrast with a surrounding wilderness, and be, as it was grand and horrible, a charming and enchanting Circe, who gave draughts of intellectual pleasure to the beings that resorted to her shrine.

The reader will pardon this—the extravagance of the moment which I attempt to describe—and allow me to inform him that this was the young lady introduced to his notice at the beginning of this chapter.

CHAPTER V.

—— When some writer in a public cause,
His pen, to save a sinking nation, draws,
While all is calm, his arguments prevail;
Till power, discharging all her stormy bags,
Flutters the feeble pamphlet into rags.

SWIFT.

WE must now be content to leave Ellen (for this was the name of this person), on a visit to the gay and gossiping town of ——, where my father dwelt, in all the greatness of a fame which an ex-lord-chancellor awarded him when, at the bar, he called him *the flower of the ——shire attorneys.* His temperament, always sanguine, was now bubbling with excitement; and, as the cause of this intimately affected me, both then and afterwards, I shall lay it down as briefly as possible.

A letter, written by a talented innovator, published

in the interesting form of a shilling pamphlet, and
laid out to catch the popular prejudices against the
Church Establishment, had been addressed to the
highest ecclesiastic in the diocese. To this letter I
had ventured *a reply*, and having transmitted the
MS. to my father, left it to the exercise of his discretion, when I went away into Scotland. With all
the partiality of a parent, he had sent it, with unmixed confidence, to the press; and now the fer-
ment, produced by its appearance, was leavening the
whole lump of the good folks, not only in our town,
but in those for some miles round. In fact, such
was the enthusiasm, that my fortune was considered
made, and the conclusion was, that, notwithstanding
some little irregularity (the consequence of partial
blindness and elevated plebeianism,) in my college-
testimonials, and a considerable difficulty in getting
a title for orders, I had only to place myself, an
accredited author and champion, before the prelate,
and he would ordain me. This, I say, was the unc-
tion with which my good friends cheered me.

It was to prosecute the designs of which this was
to be the consummation, that I was so strenuously
invited home; and, after having been cruelly disappointed in my anticipations of an interview—or at
least an interchange of notes—with Ellen, and having
thrust my things into my portmanteau, I took my seat

on the roof of the mail, the most comfortless (save in the advantages of quick travelling) of all conveyances. A long and delightful evening was favourable to meditation; and, whether I thought of the bishop or of the beauty; pamphlets or love-letters; orders or matrimony; my mind was in an admirably placid frame, and every thing seemed to follow my wishes in most perfect acquiescence.

I had received no answer to my note; but then it might have been intercepted; or, engaged in the attention due to a prior claimant, the young lady might probably have yielded to prudence (alias prudery) what was denied to romance. I blamed myself for not having entered into some account of my pretensions. I had relied upon the idea that every thing pertaining to, or consequent upon, circumstances so singular as those detailed in the preceding chapter, should be done in an out-of-the-way style; and, while I felt that I was sincere and passionate in the performance of my Romeo, I forgot that my Juliet might not have caught the fire of unsuspecting love.

However, though many surmises crossed my mind— some, indeed, turning on the possibility that the heart, as well as the outward circumstances, of the *nymph of the storm* (as B—— and I had designated her), might be averse from me and my offer; others, that, as I had never appeared to her but in the doubtful light of (at best) a pedestrian-tourist (though I cherished an idea that my altered appearance was scanned through the blinds during my long saunter in front of the Episcopal chapel), I had no right to conclude that she thought me worthy of her hand—I was nevertheless bent upon rejecting all obstacles and adhering to my passion, 'mid all the graver concerns which called me for a time away.

We had ascertained the name, condition and circumstances of Ellen, from the landlord of the inn, at which we tarried not only the night, but during the day and night following, after the adventure of Ben Lomond. For this worthy Boniface (Stuart was his royal name, and his house on the side of a sweet little loch, not far from another lovely water—the scene of *the Lady of the Lake)* had readily consented to *lionize* us by the fire-side at the expense of our company; and we as eagerly entered into such a mode of passing the greater part of a night in which sleep was murdered by the vision which occupied our minds, and the recollection of the no less, but otherwise, stirring events of the past day. We were indeed, a droll pair of *knights-errant,* in each other's estimation, as we sat devouring the legends of the lakes and hills, and quaffing gaily the well-earned rewards of " toils and dangers o'er." There we were, dressed out from head to foot, in the raiment of Jemmie Stuart—we herring-gutted striplings, he being a noble, well-paunched representative of the good cheer for which his house was famed : B—— adorned in a coat and vest of divers colours, according to the clan of our host, cut in the style of a half-century ago, with goodly silver buttons, not only where we yet retain them, but on the waistcoat-pocket flaps which lay upon his retiring thighs,—I, in a roomy boating jacket of shaggy blue, with trowsers (to match, in capacity) of even coarser and warmer flannel. Thus we sat, one in each corner and Boniface between us ; while the rest of the household were actively and cheerfully employed in washing and drying our proper habiliments, for the morrow—the *gude wife* condescending occasionally to throw in an interjection, the object of which was either to correct her husband's tendency to the marvellous or to compliment the sagacity of her guests ; and, not unfrequently, *to tak' a drap* of consolation under the unusually and unreasonably laborious task in which she had consented to forego the enjoyment of rest.

Well—as all these things, when recalled to mind, played about the current of my thoughts, I remembered that the landlord Stuart told us of the fair one ;—that she was the elder daughter of the house and heart of her father, a respectable Highland gentleman-grazier ;—that she had been educated in one of

the first " establishments" in Glasgow—was as amiable as she was *bonnie,* and the pride and admiration
of all the country round—" and I ken," added the
worthy man, with a politeness, mixed with good-
humour, which gave sufficient instance of his high
descent, " that ye are na the furst, by mony, wha ha'
fa'n i' love wi' bonnie Miss C——ll; and here's to
your health, and my service to ye, jontlemen."

We were relieved, moreover, from much mystery by
the intelligence that what we had conceived to be a
hamlet was, in fact, only one house made up of
many ; and that, had we stepped in, (as, indeed, we
were invited, but from a sort of panic had declined,)
we should have found the arrangements within in
perfect contrast with the outward appearance, mysti-
fied as it was by the torrents of rain to which we had
been exposed and could give testimony.

When thoughts of this more felicitous kind gave
way to speculations on my future profession, I was no
less disposed to view things with a single eye, seeing
in Bishops every thing that was grave, benevolent and
good ; and anticipating, in the whole body of the
clergy, an active and healthy circulation of brotherly
kindness, helping one another, and capable of any
thing but of not loving one another :—

> " Just men they seemed, and all their study bent
> To worship God aright."

Of myself, I thought, or rather, never doubted, that the qualities essential to a clergyman were in my composition. I was alive and open to all the wants and infirmities of my fellow-creatures—I could soothe and console them in their distresses; and, when it should be permitted me, I would win them to the love of holy things by an ingenuous zeal in their behalf. A great-uncle of my father had been a clergyman; and from what I had heard of his character, he was the pattern which I had placed before me, and the rivalry to which I aspired was to equal him in the posthumous praise which was conferred upon his memory, by Dr. Watson, then Bishop of Llandaff, in some lines upon his monument, which I here transcribe, partly through a natural vanity, but partly (and especially) because they explain the ideas I had of the clerical character, and are an exquisitely beautiful specimen of first-rate elegiac talents.

" Amidst a flood of sorrows bursting forth,
    Speak, grateful friendship! gentle * * 's worth;
    With steady faith, each movement to controul,
    Dwelt piety, the inmate of his soul.
    Ne'er did his soul from virtue swerve aside,
    With learning stor'd, yet free from learning's pride;
    Rewarding plenty bless'd his calm abode,
    And wisdom's right hand length of days bestow'd,
    When nature droop'd, oppress'd with slow decay,

Mild-beaming hope illum'd his setting day;
Around his couch soft-whisp'ring comfort stood,
And peace—attendant only on the good.
Her faithful herald did Religion mourn,
And * *, hapless village, wept forlorn.
But, though for ever silent is the tongue
On which persuasion's sweetest accents hung,
That bade the sinner grace's call obey,
That charm'd so oft despondency away,—
Though nought could rescue from the ruthless grave
His heart that sympathiz'd—his hand that gave;
Yet shall the truth recording marble tell—
How lov'd he liv'd, and how lamented fell."

My ideas of the *Church* were then such as were put forth in my letter to the bishop's *invader,* and such as I am proud to acknowledge yet. I was ready to defend her *ministers,* for, though I knew little of them, that little contained much less of evil. Her *liturgy* I could even more readily defend, because I knew what its effects had been on my own mind, and how often unruly passions and inordinate affections had been subdued and chastened in the chapel of our college; and I remembered how, in childhood and succeeding youth, my devotion had increased with each participation in its service. Added to these impressions, the sanctifying influence of her long-drawn aisles and cloistered courts upon my imagination, had made me, what I professed to be, a zealous champion of her institutions; and, while education and habit had made me a churchman, my judgment had convinced me that, as far as this age can be compared with that in which the Gospel was announced to the world, our establishment, her ministry, and her forms of worship, were in accordance (with very few, and these not general, exceptions) to the spirit and intentions of Christianity. *Dissenters* I viewed with a perfect indifference, except that I wondered how men could differ from what was so palpably desirable, and attributed the departure of the multitude from the church to a want of information and an innate love of change, connected with that self-important, all-sufficient disposition to judge for himself, which perhaps characterizes the uneducated Englishman. That dissenters should abound in a country like ours, worked up to the highest pitch of national pride and importance, was no wonder. Many there are, no doubt, whose difference is in point of faith; but the great mass are nothing but political mal-contents—a division which obtains a place, because idleness and dissipation will always produce restlessness and complaint, in every community; but never so decidedly as in one which *has been* long prosperous and flourishing. John Bull *will* think for himself; and, sooner than let another appear to think for him, he will deny his own creed, and be a Dissenter. But, though it may be the effect of political distraction to weaken, and, if carried far enough, to destroy a state, yet the Church, I felt convinced, was in no danger. The spiritual nature of truth must triumph for ever, and, though the fabric may fall, its walls having been stripped, its altars polluted, and its sacred records mingled with the dust, yet the spirit shall remain unsubdued; and, as there was the Church in the wilderness, so, if England, as a human polity, should be doomed to follow in the train of Egypt, Greece, and Rome, yet, as a religious community, her Church will continue to shine even in affliction's blackest night.

These thoughts, under every possible circumstance of variation, occupied my mind, until, worn out with the night's travelling, I was glad to fold up both mind and body in the bare endurance of the journey.

All who have travelled through a summer's night on the roof of a coach, are well acquainted with the searching cold of the wind, which ushers in the dawn of the morning—how it defeats every attempt at self-composure, only to make the enjoyment greater when the god of day mounts, with his glowing steeds, the acclivity of the horizon, and visits the earth amid the chorus of a thousand songs.

CHAPTER VI.

Where thou art gone,
Adieus and farewells are a sound unknown;
May I but meet thee on that peaceful shore—
COWPER.

EVERY man, who has passed through any one of those ordeals, from the grave and important decisions of which the world receives tributary streams of professional talents or pretensions, will easily comprehend me, when I say, that the restless and fidgetty fortnight which succeeded my return, was crowned by my admission to the sacred office of a Deacon. Introducing myself to the reader in this altered character, I may be expected to say something of the *modus operandi* by which I was *outwardly* (let no one accuse me of jesting with *spiritual* things,) received into the ministry of the Gospel; but, before I do this, let

me lay before him a copy of a letter to B——,
whom I had so suddenly left in the heart of the Highlands:—

" MY DEAR B——,

" By this time you are in Edinburgh, and my promise to write is the more readily sought to be fulfilled,
inasmuch as a strong tide of selfishness impels me
to it.

" Congratulate me upon the entire restoration of all
the peace and good understanding which ever existed
between me and my father—upon, I may say indeed,
the triumph over every thing of gloom or disappointment, on his part; and this has been effected by the
success of a little pamphlet of which I now send you
a copy. Ay, in utter detestation of that worthless
class of *roués* with whom (and I may with confidence
appeal to you) I never, even in appearance, had any
connection, but in the warmest and most endearing
remembrance of those intellectual hours—those soul-
improving events—those edifying, ennobling, inspiring
conversations, the calling back of which brings with
them the name of B——, I demand and obtain your
sympathy in the real pleasure which paternal love and
solicitude have made me again acquainted with. In
the warmth of his affection, and (if I may add, without vanity,) of his pride, he calls me his *brave lad,*

acknowledges that, indeed, I never gave him real cause of anger or disappointment — in that I never failed to obtain and keep the road, though I never soared much in the air ; — laments only that my talents (as he is pleased to call them) had not been planted in the more congenial soil of a classical university—that Cam—the unpropitious Cam—had the honour of my acquaintance; and enters so fully and generously into the things which belong to me, that, with the peculiar feeling of a father, he makes them all his own. Congratulate me, I say, on these things.

" Can I ask the same suffrage on behalf of another acquisition ? ' You remember Ellen, our hamlet's pride,' — the remembrance of those events through which, like a heavenly star, she shone to guide and bless her votaries, will never die.—I am in love with her, honestly, and in the fullest sense of the phrase. I saw her in Edinburgh. I wrote to her, but had no answer. This note (enclosed), the superscription of which will inform you of her residence in town, is for the post, (have they a two-penny post in auld Reeky?) and may it, in its introduction to your hands, obtain the happy consummation of those auspices which led us jointly to that door at which we first beheld her!

" Let me now inform you that I am to be *ordained* next Sunday. A clergyman, far advanced in years and a magistrate, has been, after much shuffling and disappointment with regard to others, prevailed upon to grant me a title, *i. e.* to nominate me to the office of curate in one of the two parishes of which he is the incumbent. This nomination, as he frankly acknowledged, had been twice refused by the bishop; but as, considering his own farther progress in years with a correspondent increase of infirmity, and my late achievement, a third effort seemed more than likely to be successful, he consented to furnish the necessary document upon the terms of a covenant, which, nothing less than a desire to see such woful practices banished from the world, could have induced me to be explicit enough to state, even to you.

" For the mere *nomination* on his part, I am to do whatever duty he may require, in the said parish, for two years, *for nothing;* although, in the nomination, it is written that I am to have £80 (or is it only £50?) a-year, a consideration which I readily consented to forego, the statement of it being merely *pro formâ.* Had this been all, it were well: but, in addition, as an acknowledgment of the boon (for the other is a service to the gratuitous discharge of which I aspire) I am to be private tutor to five or six of his children, girls as well as boys.

" This is a monstrous piece of market-work. And, yet, according to our constitution in church and state, every man is compelled to go through something of the sort, (except, indeed, you ' little kings,' who enjoy the ' pretty things') unless he be fortunate enough to have that influence in his behalf which falls to the lot of only few. I have no kinsman in the church, near enough to be actuated by any feeling of partiality towards me; and every clergyman, who has a *bonâ fide* title at his disposal, has some relation (money or blood will make relationship in these bad days) for whom his privilege is in store. Can any thing be done to remedy this? Perhaps, if the bishop had the charge of appointing curates, in rotation from a list of names of all eligible candidates within their respective dioceses, much that is really self-degrading might be avoided.

" I forbear from expressing to *you* my feelings with regard to yourself—my ever best and most valued friend! but beg of you to believe me,

" Yours, very truly and sincerely,

" * *."

It should be observed that I had received, from the worthy prelate to whom a copy of my little publication had been sent, and in his own hand, a very flattering and courteous acknowledgment of the " *service*" which *I had* " *done the state*"—" *no more of that;*" and now, the Episcopal satisfaction, with respect to my papers—those sundry documents and credentials which are required, was conveyed to me by the usual functionary; so that nothing either damped my ardour, or delayed me in my journey to the bishop's palace.

On the day appointed I was there, with twenty or thirty others, whose errand was similar to mine. There old college-acquaintance was revived; there knowing intimations of my good prospects were unfurled—and, truly, when we see so many men who *have done nothing*, preferred to benefices, my vanity led me to suppose it not impossible that, on account of what I had done, (so much greater is *any* thing than nothing) something might be done for me; particularly as my antagonist had thought me worthy of honourable mention in his next edition. My examination passed off well, and I was complimented even by the examiner on my late performance; and then, to crown all, I was honoured, above my fellows, with a presentation to, and audience with, the gracious, affable, and truly venerable old man, at whose hands I was so soon to receive the divine commission.

The day of ordination came—I was invested with the orders—we all dined with the bishop: but I, the all-important egotist, was directed to a seat next but one (this was the preacher) to the prelate, who honoured me with many marks of attention and with a very considerable part of his conversation.

The world acknowledges this exalted churchman to be an amiable, venerable, and Christian man; and, as my own feelings (notwithstanding some philosophical attempts to neutralize the distinctions between man and man, when both are above a certain *par*) told me he was a great man, it must be owned that these condescending attentions had such an effect upon me that I felt amply repaid for my humble service, in the assurance of his favour, and sat, something (in my own feelings, if I can recall them,) like the Mantuan bard, or him of Apulia, on the *triclinium* of Augustus.

Well, bearing my honours as meekly as I could, I returned to tell the tale to an anxious circle at home; and, in a few days, to enter upon the discharge of those duties which I had covenanted to perform, and in order to which it was necessary for me (or, to speak correctly, for my father—I being now utterly unable to earn a shilling) to be at the cost of board and lodging in the village where " my rector" (in the phrase of the day) lived, about three miles from our little cure.

Had he provided these—even these—in his own house or elsewhere, I would not here complain of the hardships imposed upon young men (and they are

willingly submitted to) who have a desire, but not the
necessary interest or connection, to enter into the
ministry; but, to get nothing, to do very much, and
to be at every expense in the doing of it, was a sorry
case for one whose education had cost at least a
thousand pounds, besides the application of many
years of care, labour, and anxiety. However, that
dear man, who is now gone away into the world (to
us) to come, willingly undertook the burthen; and,
as if I were he that bare it, encouraged me with the
hope of better things. Oh! who has seen the countenance of paternal solicitude, at one time pale with
anxiety, at another, lit up with hope—now resolved
into legible characters of painful doubt, now bright
with a glow of satisfaction—all for the sake of his
son, and remains to tell the tale without a tear to the
memory of departed greatness? With feelings wound
up to no higher pitch of fearful hope—with cheeks
now flushed, now sunk, now furrowed by a tear—
did the old Roman fix his keen eye upon the dangers
of his son—a gladiator, than did he, my father, mark
my first assay in the pulpit. Yes, he is gone! He
sees not, with corporeal eyes, the stem which he
planted, now full of leaves indeed, but tossed by the
blustering winds, stung with the cold, and exposed,
single-handed, to the conflict of a sordid and selfish
world. He lived, however, (and for this let gratitude

for ever live) to see me manumitted from this volun-
tary drudgery, and rising, as he fondly thought, (and,
while he thought thereon, he wept and blessed me
absent, ere he died) in the scale of life, to an importance and respectability which ought to be the guer-
don only of a life spent in the discharge of duty, and
shall—for the affairs of men are in higher hands than
those which hold out bounties, not according to the
inward conscience, but in obedience to the outward
lure—be the ultimate distinction, even in this world,
of all who keep, through evil report and good report
—through the opposition of their own ungodly passions, lusts, or prejudices, as well as through the
disappointments we inherit from the faulty and
corrupt springs of society,—an eye upon the great
work, and specially upon the great Master-builder of
the work, we have to do.

My race—how nearly may it now be run!—thus
began under circumstances which seemed to impose
on me, at least for two years to come, poverty, obscurity, and, if I may add, that cramping influence
which a very small sphere of opportunities, darkened
by the idea of being burdensome still to the father of
a large family, was sure to have upon a mind at all
alive to the laudable desire of rising, though not *by*,
yet *in*, the world.

CHAPTER VII.

The mathematicks and the metaphysicks
Fall to them.

SHAKSPEARE.

Virtue, which breaks through opposition.

MILTON.

B——'s letter, in answer to mine in the last chapter, after duly replying to every part of his correspondent's tiny epistle, proved a budget of interest the most varied and amusing. I am in dread of being entrapped into a machinery too complicated for the simple movement of an autobiography; but yet I cannot forbear making a part of his letter the subject of this chapter.

- " After you left us, we did not stay long at Inverary. I found my pupils so determinedly bent on any thing but *reading*, that I yielded to the general entreaty (perhaps to yield to this was better than to submit to the event of refusal), that we should strike our tents, and advance further in quest of adventure, or, at least, in pursuit of novelty. We went to Inverness."

Such (let us just remark) is the business of *Reading with a Tutor during the long vacation.* The word *reading* consists of seven characters, but this *business* is taken in hand by seventy times seven; out of whom, four hundred never read at all, so as to deserve the name; and few Wranglers, I am persuaded, spring from these tours in Wales or Scotland, in Jersey or the Isle of Man, or trips to Boulogne-sur-mer or Rotterdam. The *intentions* of the *reading-men* may be very good, and the readiness of the tutors to do their part is beyond dispute; but, who would go into an opera-house to read mathematics, or venture upon 'Change with Milton's *Paradise Lost?* When they get out—young men, commonly, who have been cooped up at school or at home, and have just gained, during their sojourn with Alma Mater, a sufficient relish for the world to render the eye of parents the most wholesome guide during the long vacation of summer months—there are the fascinations of a country, selected generally for its beauty or fashion; the curiosity of finding out all the peculiarities of the place, its inhabitants, its neighbours, and its visitors; there is *rowing,* whether there be water or not, racing, in boats or on horses,—all these, and a multitude of conceivables, are against the purposes of which the father has a very different idea, and which he begins to suspect just when the son has written for money, after a lapse of only a third of the time for which the good old gentleman had already provided him.

With two or three of such *reading-men* (some parties, under crack-men, consist of from six to twelve; and they pay Mr. Wrangler about 30*l.* a-piece, besides all expenses), no wonder that friend B—— was glad to flow with a stream, pleasant enough to a mind like his, and not to be checked without the danger of an outburst far more to be dreaded than the consequences of its own bubbling course; and, while his *eléves* were investigating the theory of spheres upon a quadrilateral surface of green cloth, solving the adfected quadratic of a breakfast-table *a la maintenant*, or studying projectiles with the aid of a fowling-piece, not unwilling to indulge his own *penchant* for the curious or sublime. He writes as follows:—

" In our retreat from Inverness, not choosing to come, as we went, by the Caledonian Canal, we travelled by Badenoch to Perth—a journey of nearly 120 miles, which we performed within a week, giving ourselves time to take almost every opportunity of visiting the most remarkable places in the *route.*

One's feelings undergo great and too violent changes —the excitement kept up is too great to allow the life of a tourist to be a long one. For instance, a portion of the early part of our road lay through a pass called Slochmuichk, renowned by many stories in the mouths of the oldest inhabitants, for acts of daring, worthy of the most relentless banditti of the Abruzzi, and no farther back than the middle or latter part of last century. One of these stories, which is, I believe, well authenticated, I cannot forbear relating to you—it affords so much cause of wondering interest.

" One Mackintosh of Borlum, a man of superior station, good education, and winning address, was, as is notorious, connected with a gang of desperadoes which infested this pass; and, by means of great tact and an air of French politeness common to the superior Highlanders of that time, managed to conceal his practices from his friends and live without suspicion, under the twofold character of a Scotch gentleman and a chieftain of Highland banditti. His final exploit was an attempt to rob Sir Hector Monro of Novar, after his return from India, and in his journey Northwards in 1770. In this he was discovered, and compelled to fly his country. He is said to have sailed for America, and to have fought in the war under General Washington; and we were told

that he revisited his native country some years ago.
Three of his confederates, one of whom was his
brother, were taken and hanged at Inverness.

" The next subject of interest was *Loch Inch*, in
which is found the large fresh-water muscle containing the Scotch pearl ; and with this I may connect
our visit to, and ascent of, Cairngorum, not far from
it, the surface of which, in some places, is sprinkled
over with the crystals of the name, said to be, as
they most surely must be, washed down from cavi-
ties in the rocks. They are met with, I believe, in
many other mountains, the quite white and pinkish
being the most common, and the latter passing under
the name of amethyst. Scotch beryl, and topaz, are
also found on this mountain ; but more abundantly
in the sand of the rivers Dee and Don, on the other
side of the Grampians. Thus have we, in our own
island, not only stories of banditti peculiar to the
west of the old continent, but likewise pearls and
precious stones so universally attributed to the East.

" The scenery about this part of our route was mag-
nificently wild and beautiful ; but it is very dangerous
in stormy weather. A party of soldiers were nearly
lost some few years ago, and many of them never
recovered from the effects of cold and fatigue. A
most awful occurrence, we were told, took place in
the forest of Gaick, on new-year's day, 1799. Our

informant was an old Highlander, with a silvered head and beard; and he gave the account on the faith of his own personal evidence, having been servant to the chief man among the sufferers. A party of hunters, in the company and attendance of a gentleman named Mackpherson, proceeded the last evening of the old year, that they might be out early in the morning in pursuit of deer, to a hut, or *bothie*, in the hill. A tremendous storm of thunder, with a heavy fall of snow, came on; and, in the morning, the hut was entirely destroyed, the stones scattered about in every direction, and every inmate dead. The accident has been attributed by some to an avalanche of snow from the adjoining height; by others, to electricity; and by others again, to causes of a much blacker and more fearful character. Their gun-barrels were found twisted, which speaks strongly in support of the opinion that lightning was the instrument of destruction.

" On the north side of Loch Ericht, we visited a cave, in the mountain Benalder, in which Prince Charles Stuart found refuge for a short time during his wanderings.

" I must not forget to inform you of an event which, however laughable, might have been serious beyond description, which occurred on our passage to Inverness, and about the middle of Loch Ness.

I was amusing myself with a game at chess below
deck, when, suddenly, a general cry of ' two men
overboard !' was heard from every part of the vessel.
I lost no time in running up upon deck, and, to my
great surprise, soon beheld one of my men conflicting
most manfully with one of the powerful wakes which
the paddles left behind them.   I had no fear, it was
R——, and he swims, as you know, like a duck;
but the other, of whom, in a few seconds, R——
had taken possession, while the wheels were stopped
and the boat lowered to receive them, seemed to be
in a horrible fright and perfectly unconscious of any
floating properties he possessed. Puffing and blowing,
his agony was evident ; nor can I imagine a wretch, with
a shark at his heels, and no impossibility of escape,
showing more of consternation and terror ; while
R——, on the contrary, was evidently on the broad
grin, and only called out, ' Come, shove out the
boat, my lads !'   All was soon and safely ended ;
and the dripping heroes were both put to-bed, until
their trunks could be unpacked, and new rigging (for
I must have nautical *parlance*) obtained for them.
This was a necessary observance, because we had
many ladies on board, who all took a lively interest
in the catastrophe, and expressed great thankfulness
that, at least, one of them had not been drowned.
But, the cause of all this ?   Y—— (the best reader

I have, by the way, and who has never, like the others, wholly given it up), offered to lay a wager with R——, that he (R——) would not obtain the same favour (by hook or by crook) of the lady he had had for his partner at a rubber, which he (Y——) would from her that had been *his*. R—— took the bet; and not one minute had elapsed before both had accomplished their boast. But Y——, though he lost his wager, was not allowed to go *scotfree*; for the brother of his fair partner, (a young man of about his own age,) seeing the *liberty* taken, immediately stepped up and discharged the dregs of a glass of cold brandy-and-water in poor Y——'s face. ' What shall I do?' says he (aside) to R——; and R——, equally *sotto-voce*, replied, ' Throw him overboard— I'll get him out.' This advice was taken, and in one instant the indignant Scot was paying his personal addresses to the waters of Loch Ness, R—— jumping after him with all the matter-of-course agility of a greyhound after a hare. The occurrence amused all for the remainder of our passage; and, had we staid long enough at Inverness, I doubt not we should have found it bruited there with nearly equal universality. There was something said about ' satisfaction ' and ' going out,' but R—— made a joke of it, saying that he never fought except he had the choice of *element;* and, conceiving that it would be

unfair to take advantage of one so inexpert in swim-
ming, regretted that he could not fight to retrieve
his friend Y——'s character, as he had already ex-
erted himself to save the life of his maudlin antagonist.

"Perth is a handsome city, with a beautiful site—
interesting as the scene of the Gowrie conspiracy,
and of the first exertions of Knox, the Reformer;
and, ascending Moncrieff Hill, you will be delighted
with one of the richest and most extensive views in
Scotland, and, in the contemplation of it, will be able
to appreciate the force of that burst of admiration
with which the ancient Romans, on passing over the
same ground, exclaimed upon the river and plain
beneath them—'*Ecce Tiber! Ecce Campus Mar-
tius!*'

"Here we staid three weeks, and something was done
by every one of my three pupils in the way of reading; though, if called upon to report progress, I
should fear for the result. It is a pity; but what can
one do? Certainly all they do is so much more than
they would do if left to themselves; and perhaps,
therefore, time and money are not wholly thrown
away. Certain it is, moreover, that they are seeing
the world, making some acquaintance with a most
interesting part of their own island, and gaining a
knowledge of men and manners; and this may very
likely be of more advantage to them in after life than

many *mathematics*. But a good deal is forced into them, *nolens volens*, in the course of our colloquial hours, and I endeavour to make them, at all events, *appear* once a day.

" *Fame* had heralded to my observation the news of your performance, even before I received the pamphlet which you have been so kind as to send me, and I was glad to find that you had broken a lance with ' the Northern bravo,' as my correspondent in London calls him. Poor Mother Church! She has enemies both many and mighty; but what is this more than we ought to expect? In fact, there is reason, both great and well founded, why we should hail the shout of the enemy as a token of worth in the establishment they assault; for, when did that which was worthless, or even very bad, ever sustain the shock or opposition of the world? The path of virtue is that which is rugged, and it is through stormy and deep waters that we bring to our shores the most costly treasures. Opposition, I cannot but think, is a proof, as strong as our enemies can afford, and much stronger than they are willing to admit, of the merits of our Established Church; and that there exists, now that this institution of our country is in the most healthy and active operation, such a tide of animosity against it, when the same institution, in the by-gone days of misuse and corruption, was surrounded by a sluggish pool of indifference, is a phenomenon, only to be accounted for by a serious admission of the propensity of a depraved nature to decry that which is good, or, at least, less evil than the world in which it is planted. Is it not the same in regard to private individuals? The philanthropist will have many a sneer, many an insinuation against the sincerity of his labours, and many a sneaking surmise of the indirection of his motives; but the barefaced prodigal, the worker of public misery, the confirmed drunkard—these men are *good fellows,* their *hearts are in the right place,* and every observation upon the bad effects of their principles is branded with the opprobrium of ill-nature, affected sanctity, or something worse. With these ideas, I am led to view all those things, which are usually considered to be against us, as so many arguments in our favour. The *soi-disant* ' increasing number of Dissenters,' especially when we reflect that but few of them are such upon grounds of conscience; the rising efforts of *Popery* taking place in unison and co-operation with the secession of *Protestants;* the outcry against the mere formalities of the Established Church, while at the same time, ' Great is Diana of the Ephesians!' resounds from every part of the complaining multitude: these I hold to be striking, and the more I reflect, they become more convincing, proofs of the improvement of our Church, in spirit and practice, in faith and utility, in the internal and external 'beauty of holiness.'

" But, in truth, we must recur to our Bibles, in order to be assured of the validity of these remarks, for they are not made hastily, nor without much anxious consideration. Whenever it has pleased our Heavenly Father to inflict chastisements upon nations, not only his judgments have been found to involve both bad and good, but also, it has been often the case, that these have been made to pass through the furnace before the heat of the flames has laid hold upon those. Is not the epistle of Peter conclusive upon this? 'Yet,' says he, 'if any man *suffer as a Christian*, let him not be ashamed; but let him *glorify God* on *this* behalf. For the time is come that *judgment must begin at the house of God:* and if it *first begin* at us, what shall the end be of them that obey not the gospel of God? And if the righteous scarcely be saved, (in that visitation, I conceive, which was about to fall upon the devoted city of the Jews,) where shall the ungodly and the sinner appear ?'

" Besides this, is there not a power *in the world*— a paramount and vaunting power—whose interest it is, expressly, to oppose the good, and promote the evil part of the things that are in the world? If not, I have grievously misunderstood the various declarations which involve 'the Prince of this world,' who *has nothing in the Lord,* 'that old serpent, called the Devil, and Satan, which *deceiveth* the *whole* world.' These, and many other expressions in Scripture, prove, if they prove anything, and, surely, not one of them is written to *return void*—that there is an opposing principle, in the very organization of the world as it is, which sets itself continually against advancing piety, improving, edifying, increasing usefulness. *Vox populi vox Dei* is a heathen motto which cannot be transferred to Christianity. In the division of that which is confessedly corrupt, the greater part should certainly contain the less warranty of good; and the grand secret why our pure form of Christianity has so many supporters, is to be found in the divine promises of succour and protection—not in the opinion of those who support it. The gates of hell shall never prevail against the true church; nor shall any respectable, even though it be not entirely a pure part of it, ever fall before the axe of the destroyer. Good is blended with evil in every human institution, notwithstanding it have its foundation in divine principles; and it is the *good* part—'Ye are the *salt* of the earth'—which preserves and upholds the whole,.

not the *evil*, which is a mere incubus, nourished by its fatness, and exists only because the whole lives.

" My letter is a strange medley, but, you know, *I* am a layman, and

"Your sincere friend,

"* * *"

CHAPTER VIII.

"Understandest thou what thou readest?"

ACTS.

BEING now one of the lowest order of clergymen—a Deacon, albeit with a license to preach and to discharge all sacred offices, except some few which it is not lawful for one below the order of a Priest to perform, I entered my new abode with feelings and ideas correspondently altered. Whatever men may say of the *call*, by their *trust* or *conviction*, in which all who are ordained profess themselves to be actuated, and whatever strictures may be drawn upon that subject I shall here say, for myself, that unworthy as I am, I felt, and have continued to feel ever since, an entire assurance that it was by the will of God that I embraced the ministry of the Gospel. More may be said upon this solemn matter hereafter. At present, let my attempts to inform the lay reader keep pace only with the life which I call to remembrance.

A Deacon is held incapable of *pronouncing* " The Absolution, or Remission of sins," because " the *Priest*" is the person to whom this office is ascribed in the Book of Common Prayer; whereas " the *Minister*" is spoken of on other occasions. If it be supposed that the words in the rubrick—" the Priest alone"—are the barrier to the deacon, this appears to be a mistake; for the word " alone" implies the *silence* of the people, and nothing more.

The same incapacity, and for equal reason is presumed to attend the Deacon with respect to the " prayer of consecration" at the Communion-time, and the giving of the blessing before the departure of the congregation. The Deacon, moreover, may not (as I was taught) administer the bread, though he may the wine, in the celebration of the Lord's supper.

These were all the points of difference in which my inferiority was perceptible to the congregation; but, if the reason be no better than that which is alleged, many other offices are not permitted to the Deacon, as a perusal of the rubricks throughout the Book of Common Prayer will (I must say, somewhat inconsistently) discover. Even before I had any holy orders I had read the lessons at church; as it is concluded any one may, at the discretion of the minister; but then, according to the rubrick, the minister ought to say that which is appointed to be said *before* and *after* each.

The first occasion of the public discharge of my ministry is vividly graven on my memory ; nor shall I ever forget the increased feeling of importance (I think it was not altogether *worldly* importance) with which I was permitted to ascend other desks and pulpits, and to minister before other and larger congregations. I was so far successful as to have the approving voice of (I may say) all, and, in my own estimation, had the option of being, or not, a *popular preacher.* My father would walk miles with me to any church to which I happened to be invited, and never, so long as my services were confined to the neighbourhood, did he fail of being among my hearers. How well do I remember all his anxious participation of my concern, and with what fond attention he would listen to my discourse and mark its effects upon the congregation—nay, he would contrive, sure enough, by conversation afterwards (especially when we dined with the 'squire, or the invalided clergyman) to draw forth the sentiments of others ; and then, when we returned in the evening, this was the topic of discourse. Oh! I call to mind green fields and shady lanes through which we thus " took sweet counsel together;" and stiles on which we rested (for he could not walk far without fatigue), and relieved the monotony of our converse with observations on surrounding scenery. Oh! those were pleasant days. They are gone; and so is he. No one now supplies his room—a father lost can never be replaced. I was then a child : now am I the father of children who may one day inherit those pure joys which spring from such a hallowed source.

During the week, my pupils chiefly occupied my time—the elder ones coming to me and I going to the younger ones; while an invitation to dine about once in three weeks was, I suppose, the acknowledgment of my services; and even then there was much stiffness and little brotherly kindness exhibited. A self-conceited son or two, beyond the age of Tuition, and a daughter, who thought herself an exquisitely fine young lady, gave themselves strange airs, and treated their poor old father with disgraceful contempt. I can call to mind one evening when the eldest son (and he was a counsellor learned in the law) had finished the reading of some extract from a book on the table, the old gentleman observed, pithily enough, " I have not heard one word you've uttered :" upon which he replied, with a sarcastic coolness, which cut me to the heart, " Well father, if you really will not use a syringe and plenty of soap and water, I cannot help it."

In justice, however, to " my rector," this state of things did not last long : for, one day, having probably endured some compunctious visitings, and, not unlikely, observed some dejection in my manner, (for the image of my poor, paying father, who was too little adapted to the world to obtain and keep a state of affluence, would rise to mind full often,) he handsomely· and frankly declared the engagement at an end, and allowed me to be free as the air. This, I need not withhold, was cheering to me in the extreme ; and to my friends there was ample reason why it should be highly delighting. I forthwith broke up my establishment, and once more flew, like a happy bird unscathed by the fowler's skill, to the parental home.

I had now leisure to set about improving myself in the various departments of my profession. I could read with more advantage, write with less alloy, and think with greater satisfaction, now that I was not reminded by the clank of my fetters, of a bondage into which I willingly entered, and from which, therefore, that I was so soon delivered, thanks to the worthy Rector of S——, whose liberality at the last far more than compensated to my feelings for the apparent hardness, with which he drove the bargain at the first;

and, though I had no brighter prospect than to be the
" my curate" of some other incumbent, the reward of
an approving conscience made me proud, as well as
happy, in the occasional services which I now performed, sometimes as a hireling and sometimes as a
friend, in the churches of my native town and round
about.

It had been my earnest study to read well, and I do
not blush to record here that I always read the lessons—or rather studied them—before I ventured, in
the face of a congregation, most of whom were my
seniors, to read aloud the word of God. To hear this
slovenly or flippantly done, is to fail of more than two-
thirds of the effect; and it was not without feeling
great encouragement, and also a conviction of the
consequence of such reading to the hearers, that I was
informed one had said that *my reading of the lessons
was as good as a sermon.* What a reflection does
this bring with it! The word of God is rendered
inferior to the word of man—by what? By the practice of considering the lessons (not, as they are, a paramount, but) a secondary matter. Daily experience
perpetuates and confirms the utility of my practice,
which I not unfrequently have extended also to the
psalms; and it is with a hope of doing some good
that I now take in hand the illustration of its good
and great effect. We will take the second chapter of

St. Matthew, which (for our purpose) is the first of the New Testament, and in which there is scarcely a verse which does not admit of study as to the mode of reading it, so as to ensure the proper impression in the clearest manner; though it might have been selected on account of the extreme simplicity of narrative which distinguishes it, and some might, for this very reason, deem it unnecessary to study much how to read it properly. But let us see :—

The common mode of beginning the reading of this chapter is (I am persuaded) to stand firmly and to dwell much upon the *first* word, to utter the *second* with a very suppressed voice, to give, to the *third* nearly its proper emphasis, to deny this to the *fourth*, and to clip the *fifth*, together with the preposition following, in our rapidity to arrive at *Bethlehem of Judea*. But, that this mode deprives the words of their natural power and leaves the mind of the hearer unmoved by the effect which they convey, we can, I think, easily show. Let the ordinary characters be understood to attend the word of positive import, the *italics* that of comparatively higher import, and the CAPITALS that of superlatively the highest consideration. The common mode, then, will stand thus :

Now when *Jesus* was born in *Bethlehem* of *Judea*.

But, if what we are endeavouring to do be really worth the doing, let the gentle reader consider well what weight such a sentence thus read would carry to the mind of the hearer. Nearly none. The words, however, are of the highest scriptural importance; and we suggest that they would be permitted to set forth this importance if read in the following manner:

Now. WHEN JESUS WAS BORN *in Bethlehem* of JUDEA.

Thus, the *now*, which is merely a particle of connection, like the Latin *autem*, or the French *or*, and really has no meaning at all, is reduced to its proper insignificance; while the four words following (and particularly the first of them, which gives the decided commencement, like a leader at the head of his men, to the sacred narrative) have their due importance restored to them. This emphatic declaration—WHEN JESUS WAS BORN—leads the mind, also, to the connection which it maintains with the locality of the Saviour's incarnation, and, above all, with the prophecies which so clearly foretold the event, time, and place. *Judea* should have an additional emphasis, because there was another *Bethlehem* in the tribe of Zebulon.

The following clause, also, is not unworthy of attention; for it conveys a clear allusion to the declaration of the prophet that the sceptre should not depart from Judah until the Messiah came. Now Herod was not only not of the tribe of Judah, but a *foreigner* altogether—an Idumean; and, consequently, particular stress should fall upon the word *Herod;** nor should the words on each side of it be without more than positive emphasis ;—

In the *days of* HEROD the *king,*—

for the Messiah being born in the *last* year of *his* reign—before *his* time was over—is a confirmation of the prophecy, the sceptre being justly to be considered as *departing,* not *having departed,* during the first reign of *foreign* dominion.   We lose much, if we do not recollect that the very word *Herod* would, if pronounced with due emphasis and in due connection with *king,* convey to the mind of a Jew something like what a Frenchman may be conceived to understand when told of France *in the days of* EDWARD *the king.*

The remaining part of the verse (let us go through, if so be, with our folly) would commonly be read by

---

* Herod, surnamed the Great, followed the interest of Brutus and Cassius, and afterwards that of Antony.   He was made king of Judea by means of Antony, and after the battle of Actium he was continued in his power by his flattery and submission to Augustus.   He rendered himself odious by his cruelty, and as he knew that the day of his death would become a day of mirth and festivity, he ordered the most illustrious of his subjects to be confined and murdered the very moment that he expired, that every eye in the kingdom might seem to shed tears at the death of Herod.   (*Josephus*).   Is this credible of human nature ?

a school boy, without any partiality, in one even strain—" behold, there came wise men from the East to Jerusalem." But, a moment's attention will show that *wise* requires particular emphasis, because it conveys to the mind that these were skilled in the knowledge of the prophecies relative to our Saviour's coming—such *knowledge* being the only *wisdom* among the Jews; for, as Dr. Whitby observes, "The Jews believed that there were prophets in the kingdom of Saba and Arabia, who were of the posterity of Abraham by Keturah; and that they taught in the name of God, what they had received in tradition from the mouth of Abraham." *Jerusalem*, too, requires considerable stress; for it is in opposition to *Bethlehem*, not in apposition with it, as we say, and as it would appear to be if not marked with suitable emphasis. The places were six miles apart; and the wise men resorted to the *capital*, for reasons which it cannot be difficult to divine.

Looking at the *fourth* verse—" And when he had gathered all the chief priests and scribes of the people together, he demanded of them, where Christ should be born"—would not the ordinary reader lay a vast weight upon the word *demanded*, from which he could hardly recover till he came with his hammer again to he last word *born?* But this is manifestly improper; seeing that the former word conveys nothing more than what may be collected as the purpose of the king in " gathering all the chief priests, &c. together." Rather, instead of the common mode,—

he DEMANDED of them, *where Christ should be* BORN.

let it be read thus :—

he demanded of *them,* WHERE *Christ* SHOULD be born :

for, what is their answer? " In Bethlehem of Judea."

Again, in this verse (5th)—" And they said unto him, In Bethlehem of Judea : for thus it is written by the prophet,"—how readily should we rob the little word *thus* of its force, and carry it to *prophet,* if we did not consider that the following verse, in which are the words of the prophet, hangs upon this *thus;* and that we ought to read it, pausing after *thus,* in such a manner as to give the following sense :—

For it is written by the prophet *thus*—" And thou Bethlehem, in the land of Juda, art not the least among the princes of Juda : for out of thee shall come a Governor, that shall rule my people Israel."

Passing to the 8th verse, to read,

" And he *sent* them to BETHLEHEM,"

would very likely cause the hearer not to notice that it was in consequence of what the chief priests and scribes had told him about a prophecy of which he neither knew, nor cared to know, any thing, that the king sent them to that place. Better, surely, thus :—

" And he SENT them *to* Bethlehem—"*
The royal mandate, in this verse, might be read, with good effect, in such a manner as to convey, if possible, the craft of that *old fox* ; and, if it could have been brought to the stage, Kean would have given it a stirring power. But, though the gravity of the desk would not permit the scowl, the affected urbanity, or the lying, designing barefacedness of the passage, much might be done; and, if any improvement can be suggested by the following, the writer of this will be too happy :—

" And said, Go—and *search*—DILIGENTLY—for the young child; and—when ye have *found* him (these words in a rapid style of indifference) *bring*—ME—*word* again,——that *I*—may come and WORSHIP him *also.*"

In the 11th (despite of what Johnson has done) I would put the accent upon the second syllable of *frankincense.*

In the 12th, " And being warned of God in a dream, that they should not return to Herod, they

---

* *Exempli gratiá,* a dialogue between A. and B.
A. What's to be done this week, B. ?
B. Well, I don't know—its York festival, is it not ?
A. Right, B—, and let us GO *to* York.

departed into their own country another way," surely, the emphasis (after the intimation of the interference of God, which, I need hardly observe, should be read with clear and distinct gravity) is divided between *not return to Herod* and *another way*. After the direction to flee into Egypt, given by the angel to Joseph, in the 13th, no one would deem it advisable to lay a stress upon *Egypt* in the 14th. " And *was* there" is in reference to the angel's instruction above—" And *be* thou there;" and ought, of course, to be read accordingly.

In the 16th, a nice sense of propriety might be discovered by reading so as to let " *all the children*" be carried, through the intervening " that were in Bethlehem, and in all the coasts thereof," to " *from two years old and under.*"

In the 18th, every body knows the meaning of " because they are not," that it is not, " because they are not *comforted*," but " because *they are* not (in existence)," the tyrannical monster having ordered them to be slain.

By an attention to this mode of scrutinizing the lessons, and making them *my* lessons, I flatter myself I am daily instructed and tend in some degree to the instruction of others. At all events, good reading commands attention; while a bombastic method of running it over, like the letting go of a chain-cable, too often disgusts,—a slovenly recorder-like, or clerk of assize-like style, is sure to offend,—and an inaudible mumbling is any thing but an exemplification of the proverb, "*Omne ignotum pro magnifico.*" I shall insert two instances which have always struck me as peculiarly entitled to attention, and shall mark them as (I conceive) they ought to be read.

"O FOOLS, and SLOW—of heart—*to* BELIEVE—all that the prophets have spoken!" (Luke xxiv. 25.) "*I* am ONE that *bear witness* of myself, *and the* FATHER that sent me *beareth witness* of me," (John viii. 18.) I am one, and the Father is another—thus there are two witnesses.

CHAPTER IX.

Of joys departed, never to return,
How bitter the remembrance!

Unknown.

WHILE "in want of a curacy," I was informed of
" a situation" in which the duties of an absentee
were to be performed in a village of one of the next
counties, for *a guinea and a half* per week, and the
privilege of residing in the Rectory-house. I applied
and was appointed.

The honour of personating a Rector was not to be
denied ; and I now remember the glow of self-importance, if you like, but it was that better sort, which
fills the breast with gratitude, and makes it beat high
with noble purposes—which animated my steps as I
walked into that pretty parsonage, beneath the salute of
a cold-looking, middle-aged housekeeper, whose attentions to me and my wants were something like those

which the grandees of a city may be supposed to pay to their official *prefect*. They were paid to an *office* at least next akin to that of her own master ; and though while she remembered that I was *only a Curate,* she might say within herself, " *Poor soul ! I reckon he's somebody's bairn,*" her demeanour was decidedly that of an inferior.

Here things went on well. I found a little library at my service ; and, as I entered in the winter, the opening spring cheered me with those promises which are the more gladly embraced because they never fail of being fulfilled. Come frost, come snow, come cutting winds, still, in due time, the fields are verdant, and the summer woods wave on high. I remember to have thought something of myself when, in college rooms, I sported my oak, stirred my fire, and drew my table to the sacred hearth; but I seemed now to have a *house* of my own ; and when I returned from my morning walk of duty or of pleasure, or of both, I rubbed my hands with an involuntary feeling of delight, as I sat down to the repast prepared for me.

So fully, indeed, did my affairs impress me with the idea of *domus*, that the *placens uxor* fell naturally into my mind. I had long and solitary evenings ; the supply of my wants seemed hardly to warrant the ceremony of answering the bell, and I, therefore, felt the more satisfactorily that it was not good for me to be alone. Now and then, a parishioner would be prevailed upon to come in and talk of horses, corn, *et id genus omne*; but then, such was a kind of society which made the lack of it more striking. He would ask, with a mysterious air, the price of the wine I gave him, or enter into some *reckonings* about the pecuniary part of my engagemènt; and, indeed, I could see that the housekeeper felt some scorn when she beheld, certainly not her better, exalted to a seat in the dining-room.

Naturally enough the reader will suppose that the Highland fair one received no small portion of my thoughts during the hours which were fairly claimed from the more bounden duties of my vocation, and truly so; notwithstanding much had been said and done which, if it had not weakened, had at least clothed in other colours the attachment which yet nestled in my breast. During my stay at home, the subject, which had been revealed by degrees, was often discussed between my father and me; and the letters which, after the ice had been once broken, flowed one upon the other from the accomplished pen of Ellen, with a welcome regularity, did not all escape the perusal of that eye to which they were submitted, with more of duty than of cheerfulness, on the part of one dependent yet for much upon a father's bounty.

The first letter which I received was certainly *cold,* when compared with my fervent epistles, but sufficiently warm in those expressions of courtesy and good humour with which every female knows so well how to receive the first addresses of an admirer. I was "pleased to say" a great many things, and my "partiality" led me into, it was feared, "a too flattering estimate" of her "humble pretensions;" but, yet, it was a greater pleasure to me to trace in it that I was not alone pleased in the matter of these "polite and elegant epistles"—the designation given to my outpourings; and, perhaps, had there been less of coldness in the reception I met with, there would have been less of ardour in the perseverance with which I continued to ply my pen. There is, however, nothing sacred without mystery; and, in the acknowledgment of my suit, there was a cloudy ambiguity, the shadow of which was cast over all succeeding letters—an *aliquid amari,* which gave a *twang* to all the rest—a something which I was at a loss to unravel, about "inauspicious rivalry" and the "sacred claims of friendship;" and, in spite of my entreaties—in spite of all my efforts to obtain a candid and avowed acceptance, before all others, in the good graces of my fair correspondent, I remained, at the time I am writing of, in as much uncertainty as ever.

It was certainly under the influence of this mystery that I had begun—may I say it?—to waver. The canvass, under which I had hitherto so gaily braved all opposition, began to flap in the shifting wind; and I almost brought myself to believe that I must, after all, contemplate the abandonment of all my projected hopes of bliss. I had learned, from her own avowals, that my ladye-love was, and would be, portionless; but this (and my passion had neither origin nor continuance under the idea of any thing else) was not the cause of wavering. It was the mystery that, though my letters were well received and, at last, affectionately responded to, I never had succeeded in extorting a confession that, as she was to me, so was I to her, the sole object of that which is commonly called *love*. The capriciousness, perhaps the coquetry, which too often waits on beauty, and the natural wisdom of remaining free to embrace the golden opportunity, by refusing, like a cautious voter, to declare her choice, were imputations which would often steal out, and fix themselves upon the fairer portion of mankind; and, whatever other thoughts might have operated on my feelings, it is candidly admitted that, under the every-day influence of *substance versus shadow*, I one evening fairly acquiesced in the vulgar adage, and concluded that, being *both* poor, an alliance might be a real injustice to the lady, and a source of mortification to us both; for, as the ready monitor insinuated, if to be obliged to sustain the character and appearance of a gentleman upon the scanty income of a curate were bad enough for me alone, what would become of me with the appendage which comes with that little but important monosyllable which, as Peter Pindar has it, rhymes with *strife?*

Let me, however, endeavour to escape the wrath of any fair reader who may honour these pages with a perusal, by pleading, if not *the general issue,* the imperious law of necessity, in my behalf. I never ceased to love—nay, in the midst of my most *prudent* cogitations, when, with legs outstretched, and eyes screwed to the lineaments of glowing embers, I pondered over and over the *ways and means,* her sweet countenance, with its pensive yet joyous expression, would seem, by its ideal presence, to dispel all grosser schemes, and win me back to the homage of the heart. If I walked in the field, and, as the fat acres called to mind the wealth of others, thought of the littleness of my estate, there her light gracile form, with bounding step, would portray the freedom of the soul, which neither poverty nor even want should restrain: or, if among the woods I rambled in more boyish mood, those soft yet bright eyes would seem peeping through the trees to consecrate the shade, making me a pilgrim at a shrine where, though I must not, yet fain would I bow.

In earlier days, I had known the daughter of a London broker, estimable and virtuous as her father's coffers were potent and alluring. She was well-taught and well-mannered; but her parents were Londoners, (strictly so called,) without any knowledge but that which had enabled the one to get, the other to save, money, and by which the whole Babylon lay before the mind's eye of Mr. —— as a map, and any map would have lain beneath the glance of *madame,* as the *mystery* of *-confusion.* The streets, the squares, the public buildings of the metropolis, were well known by them; but a *village-curate* was known to them only as the underling of a clergyman; and, though they told me the meaning of " F. P.", that B.A. or M.A. conveyed a claim to academical equality with Rectors and Vicars, was to them as the import of the characters inscribed on *Cleopatra's needle.*

But, forbearing this semblance of severity, let me acknowledge that they had always treated me with hospitality and kindness—and that is something in London—and, above all, that their daughter was ever esteemed for her quiet, unassuming gentleness of bearing, coupled with a studious disposition to make all around her happy. There was, in her manner, none of that reluctance (whether the effect of affectation or of ill-nature) which renders so many of our accomplished vocalists and pianists any thing but graces to the lovers of the song; nor was she forward in the display of talents so well calculated to give pleasure. If asked to play, she played; if to sing, she had no hoarseness : and yet it was not the affectation of good breeding, but evidently the proof of a temper naturally sweet and well regulated by education. But, certainly, in comparison with Ellen, she would have sunk into nothing, but for the good qualities of her mind, and the substantial props of her father's wealth. Scotland's metropolis held a gem which, by its lustre and brilliancy, disarmed one of all disposition to question its internal value; while that of England owned a pearl which, though of great price, had no very daring attractions—that was a divinity (if I may use, for a moment, the unhallowed phrase of the impassioned); this a mortal—that shone unsullied in the romance of nature; this, equally pure in itself, was dimmed by reality, and, at present, this was sufficient reason why judgment triumphed over imagination, and my cherished contempt of worldly things was forced into submission to the tyrannical code of expediency. Though an arrow would pierce me at the moment I finally renounced my Ellen, yet, if I turned my back on the daughter of Dives, I looked into a cavern which, though illuminated by

the presence of a beautiful enchantress, presented the
uninviting form of the consort of Lazarus — grim
Poverty, also.

Under these sensations, I made an offer—alas! how
bitterly did I lament the policy which drove me to
the offer of all that is good in the heart—all that
Astræa left behind her—to the sordid shrine of all
that is evil in the world! I sacrificed love — the
pure, the innocent, the winning love—to interest; and
having performed the rite, returned from the idol a
miserable, self-condemned, self-degraded apostate.
In my acceptance of those maxims (*prudent* as they
are called—oh! how I hate that word!) which mam-
mon lays down for our guidance through life, I
forgot the dove-like harmlessness which confides in
the providence of Almighty goodness. Judas-like,
the pieces of silver had glared in my aching sight,
but the heart was torn and rent with misgivings,
which convinced me that what I had done was not
for my good.

My reader will excuse me from attempting to give
an outline of those elaborate letters—the one to advance my new project, the other to make apologies for
the desertion of my old one—which were addressed
to the two young ladies now brought to his acquaintance. Midway between the two capitals, I was, myself the victim of a necessity which, like the furious

foe that drives the wretch, at the point of the bayonet, into the ocean, goaded me to the proscription of my dearest feelings. Behind me was the land I loved—the native land of my love; but poverty, and sneers, and frowns, and turned-up noses, (bah! dirty trash, to drive men from their nobler reason), formed a phalanx too formidable for resistance, and I rushed forward to the element which, as it promised to save me from my pursuers, *was* hereafter *to be loved.* We read of christian martyrs who, rather than give up the lamp of truth, were hurried into the darkness of an agonizing death; and, though the comparison must be made under circumstances of extreme distortion, my adhesion to the claims of the world, drove me before the misery of deserting my (until now) loved Ellen into the greater misery of having lost her. Those holy men were forced from the edge of a precipice upon a bed of spikes below,—I stood upon the question—*How am I to live?* and the next moment fell headlong into an apostasy of heart.

Thus fallen in my own estimation, (and oh! what degradation equals this? it is *remorse,*) I trusted to the succession of events for the alleviation, if not the removal, of my uneasiness, and derived no little strength from the reflection that I had never been admitted to the entire consciousness of that supremacy to which a lover aspires in the affections of the loved.

Though *I had loved*, yet the conviction of not having caused an equal reciprocity of feeling hardened me in the determination to forget, or, rather, to love no more; and though, on the other hand, I had not yet become so ardent in my attachment to another, my heart flattered me with the assurance that it could mould itself according to the directions of duty, and would, probably, when once cast, remain more effectually and lastingly devoted.

But, amidst such temporising and moralising, and, notwithstanding the aspect of my thoughts had begun to assume an air of composure, which may be likened to what we have observed, so shortly after the execution of a malefactor, in the very place where —nay, on the very spot over which he was thrust into eternity,—who shall unfold the mental agony in which I railed at the injustice of the world—the tyrant that forces men to be liberal only that it may the more disgust them with its sordid illiberality— in plainer words, forces them to be educated like *gentlemen*, that they may be treated afterwards like *menials?* What! teach a man that he must have a will of his own, and soar above the paltry considerations of the *animal*, and then send penury to tell him that to be disinterested in the path of honour is to tread on vipers ? I ask not affluence; but let me, while my equals in talent and pretension are housed in comfortable benefices, have the portion of goods which my necessities demand; and let me not, after having ministered to the well-fed, well-paid servants of pride and luxury, go home to a fire-side stripped of its fair enjoyments—robbed of its own smiles by the reckless hands of mercenary and ungodly ——: but I will not here acknowledge all I feel—I fear no man—I fear no accumulation of present evil; but I love the partner of my lot, and I love the little innocents that hang upon our slender substance; and, for their sakes, would gladly be at peace with even that monster of iniquity—*the* world.

But, how have I been led into this digression? By the recollection of thoughts under which I read the following letter from the Highlands :—

" To this spot, consecrated by the event which gave birth to happiness—once too bright, now changed to sackcloth of hair and ashes—I returned about a week ago. My mother is dead, and we came to the funeral.

" I had not intended to betray my feelings; but this first sentence has informed you that the torrent, which I vainly strove to confine, has burst its bonds, and now, free as our mountain streams, rolls—on and on, and on,—to an ocean which—oh! I cannot name in this allegory of wordless, speechless misery, unless I call it—madness!

" I am too proud to ask of pride that solace which I now need ; but I trust I am too well-disposed towards you to be suspected of duplicity, when I add to the determination of your letter, the entire assent of

" ELLEN."

Thus fled peace of mind—thus happiness, self-murdered, died. There was a postscript to this short but voluminous note, which made my heart sink, like a dying atheist, into that unutterable state of forlorn and active misery, which it were in vain to attempt to describe. It was this :—

" I have opened my letter to add another line. I believe it is customary to return letters under a change of (feelings—this word was crossed out and supplied by) circumstances, such as the present. I ask, not for mine, but for yours ; and, like a saucy claimant, sure of my request, I have made them mine for ever. They now blaze upon the hearth to which I consigned them—they illuminate awhile our fire-side, and give a show of hospitality and comfort to the windows of our Highland solitude. Now, they are the stage for a few wild, brief, and inconstant sparks to flutter on — how busily and importantly they seem to make their several *exits*—now—now—now — they are the blackness and oblivion of the grave !"

CHAPTER X.

I thought the English of *curate* had been an ecclesiastical hireling. No such matter ; the proper import of the word signifies one who has the cure of souls.—
COLLIER ON PRIDE.

THIS "*my curate,*" said I to myself, one morning after breakfast, laying down a letter which had just been handed to me from *the principal* in London— who, while using the above expression, was conveying his anxiety that *his curate* should have every domestic comfort, in reference to a *complaint,* forsooth, which Mrs. Housekeeper had thought proper to make to her master, of the liberality with which I was assigning to my guests the worthy rector's nice little French beds,—as, indeed, I thought myself entitled to do, when those guests were my own brother and sisters ;—this "*my curate*" jars sadly on the ear—surely, there's something out of tune in it.

It was a bone in my throat. Unmeaning as it was unwarrantable, it savoured of corruption. It seemed a *stigma* upon (I have no hesitation in saying) the most worthy, most useful, most efficient portion of the ministry. The curates are the fighting men—the *hoplites* (as old Hobbs, I think his name is, has it), —whose bravery and disinterestedness conciliate and keep together the army—they are the real *pastors;* for they endure cold and fatigue and hunger, without anything, but a sense of duty, to render them anything more than mere machines—they are the living bulwarks of the church militant—as the sailor would say of his ship's guns, they are the *teeth* of the citadel. Away, then, with the arrogance of these, or the pride of those who, while they pretend to pray " for all bishops and curates," do, by their ordinary language, give countenance to that degrading and degraded idea which the vulgar have of the *inferiority* (nay, *servitude*) of *assistant-curates*, or, as they say, *curates !* Away with it ! *The curate*, as *you* call him, is one of these two characters—either an assistant or helper to the curate, or a substitute for a non-resident beneficed clergyman. In the latter alternative, his real *superiority* is evident, and in the former, his *equality* is capable of demonstration. If the *hired* clergyman owes any submission to the *beneficed* one, it is to be conceded only for the sake of unity, and not, in any case, on account of the fortuitous advantage which the one enjoys. God forbid! that while we walk, as becometh the delegates of Omnipotence, any breast should harbour a thought so pitiable, and so un-favourable to the self-respect which every man owes, and, to be a happy man, must pay.

There was a case of dispute not long ago between two Irish clergymen, which, under these feelings, I cannot refrain from alluding to. Their correspond-ence (it is not a year ago) was published. The one was a beneficed clergyman, the other did *his* duty for him. The former wrote to, and of, the latter with this offensive epithet of *my curate*, whereas he was, if any thing, the curate *of his parish*, not *of him*. But, as I wrote a letter, at the time, to the editor of the newspaper in which this correspondence was given to the public, this is what I then said, and now feel.

" Sir,—From amongst all the letters of such as, taking interest in the question of church reform, ad-dress themselves to you, should it be the lot of these few lines to obtain a place in your valued columns, I would ask if the existing state of relationship be-tween *incumbents* and (according to the language of the day) their *curates*, be at all likely to fall beneath the notice of our legislators ? for, that ' the working clergy' of the establishment labour under no in-feriority which can fairly shut them out from notice and respect, is what I shall not even suppose capable of being questioned.

" This relationship, as it exists, at present, in the public mind, is full of injustice to him who *is worthy of his hire* ; injurious to the temporal (if not, also, the spiritual) interests of the church ; and (I scruple not to add) a crying evil which would have been long since remedied, but for the meek and enduring spirit of the sufferers ; and if any ministers had ever possessed the inclination and ability which belong (it was Sir Robert Peel's) to the present cabinet.

" We all know that the expenses of an education, preparatory to holy orders, are impartial ; that talent, piety, or address is not kept in store (capriciously) for any one in preference to another ; and that there is neither reason nor equity in the position that, while two men are employed together *in the same spiritual cure,* one should be elevated to the rank of aristocracy, and the other reduced to the actual necessities of penury.

" But, yet, it is not denied that much inequality of circumstances cannot be avoided, in a world wherein the wants and desires of men are as various as men themselves.

" If, however, I should have discovered

'That stone
Philosophers in vain so long have sought,'

behold the project which has just darted across my brain. Let there be no such thing known as one inferior clergyman *under* another (both being in *full orders*). The episcopal order is, of course, to be left *over* both classes of the "inferior clergy," i. e. *over* all the *curates*. Let the *deacons*, only, be curates (improperly so called), and let them resign their deaconal office, only when promotion calls them to the *presbytery*, to which class alone let the *incumbency* (as indeed it does now, and must) belong. Death will create this promotion, *permanently ;* sickness, or necessary absence, *temporarily :* and, in this latter case, the displaced presbyter ought to possess a priority by law, and be inducted, upon proper * testimonials, in preference to any deacon.

" Such an arrangement would, of course, call for an increase of the number of *benefices,* and this must be counterpoised by the diminished revenues, both of some of those which now exist, and of the sinecure offices of the church, in such proportions as may seem good.

" Under some such modification as this, what incalculable advantages would be produced ! Simony would receive a death-blow. There would be no curates, tempted to neglect their flocks, because they

---

* I do not pretend to say what testimonials—they might embrace considerations of property, &c.

cannot, and do not, live by the *care* of them;—no rectors or vicars, deserting their charge, because they have confided it to a hireling;—no people, which is indeed a common case, disgusted with the establishment altogether, because they see the men who do the work so inadequately paid, on the one hand, or because they see the affluent incumbent, on the other, too regardless of their welfare. This is *speaking out;* but, it comes from one who is *ready* to die in the cause of the church."

And, indeed, without any breach in that bond of union by which all the hearts of those who are engaged in the same sacred work ought to be bound together, I may certainly assert that, if there be two portions of us—workers and non-workers, then the working clergy are the more efficient and more deserving members of the order; and that, if, putting aside all cases of unavoidable absence from duty, there remain not sufficient ground whereon to raise this distinction, then all are efficient and deserving, because of, and according to, their *work*.

This consideration, in addition to the justice of the case, demands a cessation of that dependence which is forced upon a class owing, by the existing order of things, to be independent of such an assumption; and this cannot be effected but by a removal of all power and superiority, really, to the hands of the bishops.

CHAPTER XI.

(*B— loquitur*) I go on in my intended Diary.
TATLER.

IN the midst of the many cares which began—at my bidding, I suppose I must admit—to crowd around my mind, I had written to thank B— for his very long and deeply interesting letter; and now it was my happiness to receive another communication from the same quarter. For two or three hours, I forbore to break the seal of it, until I was quite sure that I might calculate on the uninterrupted enjoyment of reading it. Thus capricious is the intellectual appetite. When we have coarse fare we care not how we have it; but, where the marrow and fatness of a real treat are laid before us, no observances are too contemptible to be noticed if they at all tend to the sole and undivided *gourmandise* of the banquet.

At length, the door shut, orders for dinner entirely

negotiated, and drawing myself to the side of an open, but retired and ivy-mantled window, I took the packet—the franked packet—from my pocket, conned the member's name, and brake the well-known seal.

I had conveyed to my friend some information upon the subject of my change of sentiment with regard to a consummation of my attachment to Miss C—ll, but nothing certain. I had regretted the obligations forced upon me by necessity, and complained that " the course of true love never did run smooth;" and he replied, with that frankness and generosity which had always distinguished his dealings with me :—

" I read, with much concern, your remarks—I yet hope, they are far from decisions—upon the subject of (let me say it with respect) your *affaire d'amour*. As far as the indications of a face can go, we were from the first, you know, agreed in our opinion of the lady. We had much reason to concur in the estimation of her mental qualities also, from what we heard, at Ardchinchrochdhan, from the respectable landlord Stuart; but, with regard to me, this estimation has been, almost miraculously, confirmed and vastly increased by testimony of the most indisputable order. Fallen from a high estate, and yet preserving the dignity and loveliness of female virtue such as we scarcely ever witness in the earth, she is worthy of any partner; and happy the hand which may be permitted to take her from that sphere which she almost consecrates by her presence !

" We have often conversed upon the subject of that disinterestedness in love, which (to depart for a moment from the diction of the world) is nothing but an implicit trust in the power and providence of an Almighty. I know the world is full of saws and maxims against (as they are called) *imprudent* alliances ; but, may we not soar above the world, without a crime? may we not despise its saws and maxims without a charge of contumacy? If we may not, then hang the crime and the charge, but let the accused himself turn judge and try the merits of the question. Of course, there are limitations to be applied, but the mind itself, which adopts this decision, will furnish them. It would be imprudent—nay, it would be impossible—for a man, trusting in, and not presuming upon, Almighty providence, to countenance, much more to contract, an alliance with a personification of ignorance, vice, or profligacy; but when the elegance of purity, the bright image of virtue, and the untarnished privileges of birth are centred in one, who would stoop to count the *siller,* when he has it in his power to take possession of a treasure which is inestimable? I say again, I have testimony of the highest order in favour of every real excellence which can distinguish our nature, and my only hope is that you will think again before you sail away from such a haven, to commit yourself to the Siren-song of the designing, the Scylla of the confident, or the Charybdis of the noisy, showy, and *pretending* part of womankind."

Well, thought I, this is over-shooting the mark, and B.'s noble sentiments have towered up beyond the reach of human arbitration; or, at least, out of the region of human practice. Yet, he is right.

" I promised you," says he, " another selection from my rough Diary; and, therefore, to be as good as my word, I now offer you some particulars of an excursion from Stirling, which was the next place of settlement we made choice of after Perth. It was a journey of 100 miles, for which we gave ourselves one week, extending to Fort William on the Caledonian Canal, and embracing a central portion of the Highlands almost unknown to us. Here, then, inclosed are the leaves of my Diary.

" *Tuesday.* After a hearty breakfast, of which fried salmon formed a considerable component, and a glass of Embro' ale a very grateful *finale,* we set out for Doune Castle, about seven miles on our road, without suffering any attractions to divert our progress, and cheered by the occasional song (on the part of R. and Y.) of

' Ye banks an' braes o' bonnie Doune.'

A two hours' march brought us up to this castle, the rendezvous to which Scott has represented the Highlanders carrying their captive Waverley, the English chevalier. It appears to have been built early in the fifteenth century, by Murdoch, Duke of Albany, and is a good specimen of the sturdy stronghold of feudal dignity. We lunched in the principal room of the building, which is between the two massive towers at its extremities and about twenty-five paces in length. There is an enormous fire-place in the kitchen, beneath the chimney of which more than a score persons might be accommodated, upon a pinch. There is, yet remaining, a ponderous grated gate within a heavy iron-studded folding-door, and the walls of the building exist nearly entire, though the canopy of heaven is their roof—*Sic transit, &c.*

" The early afternoon would bring us to Callender, where we had resolved to dine and spend the remainder of the day, the distance before us being nearly equal to that which we had already come. As we were informed, we found in it an excellent inn; but, like the Pharisees of old, howbeit induced by very different motives, we adjourned to a sweetly secluded spot of the River Teith, to enjoy the previous luxury of a bath—an indulgence truly grateful after a dusty, sultry walk of fifteen miles—before we resigned ourselves to the good cheer of our Boniface.

Y—— was the pledged warranty for those of us who could not swim well.

" Our dining-room window commanded a view of Ben Ledi, ' the Hill of God,' upwards of 3000 feet high; on the summit of which it was customary, in early ages, for the people to assemble, for three days in succession, to pay homage to their deity, which is conjectured to have been Baal, or the Sun : and towards the end of last century, an iron ring was discovered near the top, and made fast to the rock, by which it seems that the victims of that infernal worship were bound.   Customs, indeed, of an analogous kind have prevailed in the parish of Callender within a recent period ; and thus, our own very island almost now resounds with the dying cry of the worship of Baal or Bel.

" At bed-time, we were all four consigned to one room, in which, however, were *five* beds, two of them being, like the berths in a ship, recessed in the wall, and screened from view by snow-white curtains. What with an immoderate fit of laughing, which came, like an epidemic, upon us all, and was the more irresistible because no one could rationally account for it, and the heat of the night, we had but little sleep and that (as far as mine went) full of starts and interruptions.

" *Wednesday*.—Breakfast over, and that small portion of mathematical exercise, (not *reading*, for we had no books with us) which, wherever pens and paper can be procured, I insist on every morning, being despatched, we made a vow that we would have our luncheon at the grave of Rob Roy—twelve or thirteen miles distant, and nearly in our line of road. Accordingly we set forward, with Ben Ledi's majesty on our left hand, and more remote, on our right, the lofty hill called Uam Var. Having completed the small Pass of Leni, we walked for five miles along the bank of Loch Lubnaig, " the Crooked Lake." The hills on both sides are steep and high, and seem almost to hang over the water, their broad shadows giving to the lake a peculiar gloom which contrasted strongly with the bright sunshine overhead, and occasionally striking through some inlet. We passed Ardhullary, a farm-house on the east side of this lake, remarkable from having been the retreat of Bruce, the Abyssinian traveller, while he composed his work on that country. A few miles further brought us to the eastern extremity of the valley of Balquhidder, occupied chiefly by Loch Voil and Loch Doine; at the upper end of the former of which Rob Roy lived, chiefly, during his latter days, and at the lower end, about two miles from the public road, in the Kirton of Balquhidder, his body was interred. *Near* the grave of this bold man (for we reverenced even his ashes

more than to regale ourselves *upon* his tomb) we carried our vow into execution. The arms on his tomb-
stone, indicating his consanguinity with the royal
house of Stuart, are a fir-tree and a sword across,
supporting a crown.

" We had contemplated a small heap of stones,
pointed out to us by an old woman as the remains of
his habitation; and now, having loitered long about
the shades of this persecuted, but relentless hero, we
betook ourselves to the inn at Loch Earn-head, where
we dined, spent the evening, and slept—all in a manner answerable to the fatigues of a day full of wild
and exciting interest.

" *Thursday.*—Luib Inn was marked, upon our chart,
as the place of mid-day rest—ten or eleven miles from
the head of Loch Earn. There was nothing particularly remarkable in this morning's walk : but Glen
Dochart, through which we passed in the afternoon, is
celebrated as the scene of one of the many wonderful
escapes which Robert Bruce effected. After his defeat at Methven, the royal party, dwindled to a few
hundred men, were attacked by the Lord of Lorn with
superior numbers in Strathfillan, and compelled to retreat. Three of Lorn's men, who had by a short cut
got a-head of the king, simultaneously assailed him.
One seized his bridle, another laid hold of a leg and
stirrup, and the third leaped behind him on the

horse's back; but his undaunted courage and uncommon bodily strength enabled him, without injury, to rid himself of his three assailants.

" Further on, towards Tyndrum, there is a linn in the river, called the Pool of St. Fillan's, which is, to this day, not unfrequently the scene of the observance of a degrading superstitious rite. Every term-day, it is customary to immerse persons insane or of weak intellect at sunset. Being then bound hand and foot, they are laid all night in the church-yard of St. Fillan's, within the site of the old chapel. A heavy stick is laid on each side; round these is warped several times a rope passing over the patient's breast, and made fast in a knot, which, if found loosed in the morning, a recovery may be looked for, if not, the case is declared to be hopeless. British missionaries ! should not charity, in such cases as this and the superstitions of Callender, begin at-home ?

" This day's progress, being reported at something more than twenty-two miles, we retired for the night to a poor inn at Tyndrum, near which a lead mine has been attempted to be worked, but the project has failed. Surely the lead might be found above ground, when we see our fellow-islanders, in the nineteenth century, still clinging to the superstitions of barbarous ages.

" *Friday.*—This was a wet day, which rendered a

march of eighteen miles to King's House—a bleak
and uninteresting stage—nearly wretched. Our sorrows, however, were healed about half way, at the
public-house of Inverowran; and, by way of re-
cruiting our spirits, poor R—— took the occasion
of a stray piper and a tolerably pretty girl in the
house, to propose a Highland fling, which was well
achieved and did ample credit to all parties, as well
as to the whiskey with which it had been thought
advisable, in spite for the soaking without, to comfort
the sympathising associates within. The remainder
of the journey was undertaken *with spirit,* and the
road, lying across a tedious, high, and tiresome hill,
called the Black Mount, from the summit of which
you obtain an extensive view of the Moor of Ran-
noch, the largest in Scotland, was closed in fair
dinner-time by King's House—a solitary inn, standing
in the midst of a bleak and extensive moor, and not
particularly deserving of so royal an appellation.

" As we traversed the latter part of our journey,
the report of thunder echoing from mountain to
mountain gave a deep effect to the dreary scene ; and
as the bittern ran at our approach, or the grouse
wheeled away through the air, it seemed as if all
animals were flying a wilderness where solitude alone
was doomed to dwell.

" In the midst of our reflections, a cart, drawn by

two most shapeless animals, apparently of the pony species, appeared before us, and the strange-looking creature, perched in one corner of the vehicle proved, upon a nearer approach, to be a being of the genus Megmerriles, whose tattered and faded red cloak, betrayed a pair of high cheek-bones and a copious flow of yellow hair. R—— declared a coffin was in the cart; but, without questioning the probability of such a fact, in a district, the inhabitants of which were subject to death, though remote from even the ruder art of the *undertaker*, I must say, I saw nothing but some bundles of faggots, and, what appeared to be, a heap of soot-bags.

" *Saturday.*—That we might have an insight into the terrible grandeur of Glencoe, our day's *route* was somewhat circuitous; and, instead of pursuing the straitest cut for Fort William, we made for Balla-chulish Ferry, situate at one of the contractions of the waters of Loch Leven.* One object of interest, it would seem, was missed in our determination, to wit, 'The Devil's Staircase.' But the varied interests mixed up with the history of Glencoe rendered our passage through it a matter indispensable; and

* There is, at least, one other lake of this name in Scotland. The one I mean is near Kinross, and celebrated for its castle, from which, through the gallant instrumentality of George Douglas, the beautiful Queen of Scots effected her escape.

its terrific fastnesses, its bleak, sharp, and abrupt
crags, toppling one above the other, its wild torrents,
and, in some parts, the roof-like appearance of its
barriers, are such as, when once seen, never to leave
the mind.

"In the course of our morning's scramble, (for the
wild, broken, muddy, and ever-varying nature of our
road forbids to call it a *march*,) we stopped at a hut
to ask for water to mix with our '*mountain dew*,'
and the scene which presented itself when we entered,
baffles all description. The whole apartment under the
shattered roof was about 15 feet by 12, and this was
divided in two by a wooden fence, such as we may
see in England before the cottager's pig-sty.   In the
one (the larger) division, sat three old women, smoking with short black pipes, and faces (talk of the
witches in Macbeth !) not less black, over the fire of
sticks upon the ground.   Their age might be fourscore, over and under.   Making bread, at one side,
and beneath the doubtful light of, what appeared to
be, a window, about a foot square—some of the
small panes were green, some yellow, some black,
and others stuffed with rags—was a woman of the
middle age, with a fine figure and face *a la brunette*.
There was a sick child in one corner, in a miserable
bed, and two or three younger ones were playing and
prattling about him.   In another corner, perched

upon a table, for the sake of house-room, an older boy was amusing himself with some sort of playthings. Bare feet aud ancles was the order throughout the whole; and, as we left the hut, we met coming in, with a whip in her hand, a fine young woman, in the same costume, who appeared as healthy and as happy as their habitation seemed comfortless and dreary. But we must not leave them yet. The interior sides of the walls were so intentionally uneven in their surface, that the projecting fragments of rock (stones they were not) served for shelves, mantel-piece, and cupboards. The other division of this one apartment contained a cow and a pig; and two, if not three, beautiful black sheep dogs must be added to the forementioned *coterie*, making, on the whole, such a *tout ensemble*, that Y——, upon entering, exclaimed, in an involuntary and solemn tone, 'All hail!' The *gude wife* was like Jael of old—we asked for water and she gave us milk—and such milk! our London cream is a fool to it. A benediction sounded in our ears as we left the house, one of the party slipping a piece of money into the hand of the 'bairn' in bed.

" The history of a foul massacre, which throws a gloom over the reign of William, is attached to Glencoe. The account is this : Government had a desire to organize the Highland clans into a force for its support, and the Earl of Bredalbane was one of those entrusted with the commission. Mac Ian, chief of the Macdonalds of Glencoe, opposed himself, with all his clan, to the measure, which was, on the contrary, supported by their jealous neighbours, the Campbells—a jealousy which sprang out of the defeat of the latter at Inverlochy, by Montrose, with the aid of the former. On the successful issue of the attempt, government issued, in 1691, an order, by which all the chiefs were called upon to submit, by taking an oath of allegiance, before the first day of the following year. Mac Ian was the last to comply; but, however, before the time, he repaired to Fort William and tendered his oath to the Governor (Hill). He, not being the proper authority, referred the chief to the High Sheriff of Argyle, at Inverary— Sir Colin Campbell, of Ardkinglass. A storm of snow prevented his arrival in time, but a certificate of the oath having been taken, with an explanatory letter, was forwarded without delay. King William, on the 11th of the month, signed a mandate to destroy with fire and sword all who might have neglected the order; and on the 16th he issued a second, but containing, like the first, an indemnity to such as might have *delayed* their compliance, yet expressly *excepting* the Macdonalds of Glencoe, who were directed to be extirpated. Now for the villany. The

Sheriff of Argyle's letter was not produced to the council, and the certificate of Mac Ian's compliance was *cancelled*. Instructions were committed to Governor Hill, to the end that horrors the most savage might be perpetrated. A detachment, under the command of Captain Campbell, of Glenlyon, who had a niece married to one of Mac Ian's sons, was marched into the glen; and the soldiers, after having been most hospitably entertained by the Macdonalds for a fortnight, proceeded one morning in February to murder, in cold blood, their unsuspecting victims. Thirty-eight only were thus put to death, the majority escaping through the eastern pass, which was to have been occupied by another party of troops, but the snow prevented their arrival in time. Captain Campbell, having some years afterwards to superintend a military execution, at the time for producing the reprieve which he had received for the unhappy man, inadvertently, instead, dropped his handkerchief—the signal to fire. Horror-struck at his own fatal mistake, he exclaimed, as the man fell, " the curse of Glencoe hangs about me !"—and well might the tears of mothers, wives, and sisters, rise up against the principal actor in a real tragedy like that of Glencoe. He quitted the service in a state of extreme dejection, and, according to the popular rumour, was never afterwards heard of.

" Arrived at the Ferry we ordered dinner, and, while it was being prepared, we resolved, notwithstanding our fatigue, to visit some little islets in the basin, which is made in the lake by the contraction at Ballachulish and a similar one called 'the Dog's Ferry,' three or four miles beyond. Putting off, we soon arrived at one of them, called St. Mungo's Isle, which, as a burying-place, is divided between Glencoe and Lochabar. Here is buried the body of Mac Ian, above-mentioned; and, not many years ago, his descendants removed his ashes from the portion of Lochabar, in which he was originally interred, to that of their own clan. His bones are said to have been of great size; and his common name, Mhic Ian Vohr, 'the son of John the Great,' whence several of those who escaped, took the name Johnson, attests his bodily prowess. Indeed, in consideration of his great strength, his assassins took care to pour a simultaneous volley on him, as he lay asleep; an act of dæmoniac murder coupled with cowardly meanness, which was corroborated by the appearance of his remains, retaining many of the balls lodged between his shoulders.

" Another island, which commands a thrilling interest, is called Eilan na Corak, 'the isle of the solitary one,' deriving its name from having been chosen as the burial-place of one who had made himself an object of abhorrence and exclusion from Christian rites, by his crimes.

"We took to our oars with a silent retrospect of those scenes and incidents which were now crowding upon our imagination; and, as the same sun, which now gilded alike the resting-place of the murdered Laird, and the tomb of one excluded even by men, for his solitary vices, rose upon the deeds which they commemorate; so were we fully alive to the reflection that ONE only is just and merciful, reserving for all the bourn of that grave, in which 'the wicked cease from troubling, and the weary are at rest.' It was dusk when we arrived, and the last gleam of day threw a melancholy moral over all around us, teaching that, as 'all that's bright must fade,' so there is an end to all the workers of wickedness, after which, greatness is a word, and vice and murder retain nothing but the shudder of remembrance, or the bootless tribute of a tear.

" Near the celebrated quarries of slate, about two miles off, there is a neatly constructed Episcopal Chapel: and here we intended to worship on the following day, retiring to rest with sensations well befitting the approaching Sabbath.

"*Sunday.*— It was delightful to hear our own liturgy performed in the Gaelic tongue, and no less cheering to behold our fellow-subjects—them who had—or

whose forefathers had—so often mustered to the gathering at the voice of the pibroch—now assembled
in the worship of one God and common Father of us
all. To hear the same Maker and Redeemer glorified in a foreign tongue, gave rise to a sensation which
I never before felt. It seemed an earnest of the fulfilment of His word who says ' the Morians' land
shall soon stretch forth her hands unto God.'

" Making it a day of rest, we were content to loiter
on the banks of Leven, casting many a thoughtful eye
upon the islands of the dead, objects which possessed
an irresistible power of appealing to the best feelings
of our nature. Laird of Glencoe—murdered Mac-
donald! thine eyes were closed in the fond security
of a generous host—they opened—did they open in
the agony of that last moment?—if not, they opened
—where?—Isle of the dead! gentle is thy repose—
stout hearts have ceased to beat—is there a *mansion*
for the dark and erring brave?

" *Monday.*—We performed the remaining fourteen
miles of our journey at one stage, and, without having
been much engaged in the contemplation of any thing
by the way, entered the village of Maryburgh, con-
tiguous to which stands Fort William, about noon.
The barracks accommodate about a hundred men;
and the most striking feature of the neighbourhood is
Ben Nevis, in height nearly a mile, and measuring, in

circumference at the base, more than twenty - four. At an elevation of about 1,700 feet, this mountain has a wild tarn or mountain lake. 'The Eagle, sallying from his eyry,' says an elegant writer, ' may greet the approach of the wanderer, or the mournful plover with plaintive note salute his ear; but for these birds of the mountain, the rocky wilderness were lifeless and silent as the grave; its only tenants the lightnings and the mists of heaven, and its language the voice of the storm.'"

CHAPTER XII.

Repentance so altereth a man, through the mercy of
God, be he never so defiled, that it maketh him pure.

WHITGIFTE.

WITHOUT drawing upon the reader's indulgence by a
transcript of correspondence, I may content myself
(as I surely shall him), with observing that my new
addresses were received so far well as to keep up an
interchange of letters, the reading and writing of which
more and more increased that satisfaction of feeling
which, fanned by the wings of sincerity, already
usurping the place of interest, daily advanced to dis-
place all regrets for the loss of a prize which I had
been taught to consider myself incapable of possessing. Our nature makes excuses for us; and, in this
case, the approbation of friends tended to confirm
them all: so that, ere many weeks, I stood acquitted

by the common consent of all my reflections, meditations, and resolves. Indeed, I was led, not to rejoice in the loss of *one*, but to congratulate myself upon the access which was so prosperously made to *another*.

Reader, (especially, fair reader,) do not severely look on me as the recreant delinquent who flits from flower to flower, merely to enjoy, in the indulgence of a fickle genius, the pleasures of vanity. Pity me, if you please, as the slave of necessity, dragging a chain which my nature hated, but which my circumstances forced me, first to endure, then to seem to love.

The current of my thoughts and employments, having been for a while absorbed in the abstractions of a restless mind, returned now to their former channel; and nearly every morning saw me in the course of paying visits to the persons committed to my care, and (I say it without affectation) especially to the poor. Whether any thing like pride led me to make this preference, I know not: this I know, that such persons received me in a manner far more gratifying than the fuss and flurry of the better sort, who, in rural districts, are always for *setting you down* and *cramming* you.

I had much sickness and misery to encounter in their dwellings, even some domestic strifes, and not a few of those unhappy proofs of natural depravity,

which wring the mother's heart with that sorrow
which no one, but the mother of a daughter, can ever
feel. There were collieries hard by the parish, and
all the males of many families were engaged in the
working of them. They went down, in divisions, for
so many hours, and then came up to light for rest and
refreshment; and often I found, stretched upon their
cold damp floors asleep, two or three sons, while the
father and another child, perhaps, were in the bowels
of the earth—the mother and daughters the while preparing their coarse repast, which the addition of even
a sixpence would heighten into a feast : for I had not
then so learned, in the want of means to administer
what some would call real comfort to the poor, as I
have since been forced to learn, herein, much hin-
drance to the efficacy of the pastoral office; and, as
money was always held in some degree of contempt
by myself, not yet had I found out that it often opens
a way, otherwise so clogged and obstructed as not
easily to admit the messenger of spiritual tidings.

My income was little more than adequate to my own
wants ; and, to say I never thought of the wants of
others, were certainly an injustice ; but, if I remember rightly, I used to think and act as men would,
were the circumstances of our life so contemplated
as that it *really* consisted not in the abundance or
scantiness of the things which we possess. Among

several, there was one instance, connected with my duties, which I feel strongly inclined to place on record.

Called, one day, to visit a young farmer in the parish, who was represented to be in the last stage of consumption, I was conducted to a house about a mile from the Rectory, and soon beheld what appeared to be the last efforts of nature, in the preservation of that body from which the soul is so reluctant to depart. There was a faint and corruption-like smell in the apartment, which had been fumigated and scented so as, *intentionally*, to neutralize, but, *in reality*, so to reveal it by comparison that it struck more forcibly upon the nerve; there was the laboured breathing and the leaden eye; there were the arms laid out down beside the body, with hands attenuated; there were the sharpened features and the grisly beard; there was the sweat in drops upon the brow,—all of which (as subsequent experience has taught me, if even intuition would not teach us all) bespoke, in terms too intelligible, the approach of dissolution.

A young wife (she was his second) stood, more as in anxiously painful expectation of the event, than as in the pale, worn grief with which affection views the advent of a blow which changes the consort to the widow, and by which the children are declared fatherless for ever. In this case, there appeared to be no children. Two or three other women were in the room, sedulously, but silently, employed in adjusting and preparing those little things which, more significant in idea than in reality, prove at once the application and the vanity of human skill. Below stairs, there were two farmer's servants regaling themselves upon a mess of pottage, while (as I waited below a minute or two) a stout young woman gave her attention to something in a boiling pot. A dog lay yawning upon the hearth. But all was still. The eye alone was the medium by which every observation was to be made; for men, women, dog, and even bird in cage, were speechless, noiseless, as the fowling-piece upon the beam, or the saddle, with stirrups bright and motionless, upon the tree.

To the inquiring look of the patient, directed towards me by the motion of an old woman (alas! it was his mother) who lay half, and half leaned, upon the bed, I replied by reading, after a brief exhortation, the leading verse of the fourteenth chapter of St. John—" Let not your heart be troubled : ye believe in God, believe also in me," and some others of that and the following chapter. Then, as far as I was able, I entered into a dialogue (supported, on the part of the sufferer, by hard-drawn sighs, rather than articulations of *yes* and *no,*) upon the fundamentals of

our faith; without, however, being able to form any
notion of the state of feeling under which my observations were received, more cheering than the gloomy
one which sprang from the apparent dismay and
terror under which he laboured. My reading was
concluded with those exquisitely pathetic and appropriate compositions, the sixth and twenty-fifth Psalms;
and, not then bold enough to commit myself to the
spirit of *extempore* prayer, which has since been found
to be of paramount usefulness under such circumstances, and particularly when the afflicted are
among the most ignorant, I kneeled down by his bed
and offered up some of the petitions from the service-
book of our church. " The order for the visitation of
the sick" is, I am persuaded, better, as an introduc-
tory service where the pastoral visits are likely to be
often repeated, than any thing in any " Manual" or
" Companion" which has fallen in my way; and,
when there is a probability that your visit has been
solicited under a well-founded expectation of speedy
death, nothing can be more likely, in human hands,
to awaken, to convince, or to establish the departing
sinner.

I now took leave of a man whom I felt that I
should never see again, with a promise (contingent
upon his continuance in life) that I would see him
again to-morrow.

For several days I visited my patient, until, one morning, I was received with such altered demeanour in those whom I had seen before, that I scarcely knew what to make of it. Quickly, however, I was informed by his wife, that he was much better—so much so, indeed, that he had taken food heartily after having slept with tolerable composure. My little acquaintance with such things led me to conclude that these omens, so cheering to him and those about him, were most likely the indication of coming death. Many a cloudy evening yields to the darkness of night not before the setting sun has given " token of a goodly day to-morrow ;" and it is an observation, which I have since confirmed by some experience, that the heart is lightened and the energies seem to be revived just when the cold hand is ready to snatch us from this existence.

Without communicating any such impressions, I proceeded in a course similar to the one of preceding days; but was the more encouraged by the apparently greater interest with which the sick man entered, with much more freedom of speech, into our conversation. " You say, sir," said he, " that salvation is prepared for sinners ; but, sir, are *all* sinners able to be saved ?"

" There is," replied I, " in Holy Scripture, mention made of *unpardonable* sin—in other words, a state of sinfulness beyond the reach of even the gospel of grace and mercy; but, I can assure you that, expressing, as you do, a desire to be reconciled to God, you neither have committed the sin, nor are in this state of sinfulness. It may reasonably be questioned whether any, but a Jew of the time in which our Saviour was manifest in the flesh, could ever have committed the sin, called *the blasphemy against the Holy Ghost.*"

" I have been a very wicked sinner," now articulated the man, with eyes fixed on mine, as if he would read therein every syllable of feeling while his words fell, one by one, from his pallid lips—" I have been a great swearer," he added, in a guttural whisper. And this leading me to suppose that his mind hung upon my allusion to the *blasphemy,* for which the Scripture declares there is no forgiveness either in this world or in the next, I rejoined—

" No doubt, you have, like us all, committed many grievous sins; but let not the recollection of these, now that the world is perhaps rapidly closing upon you, lead you to any decision but that of hearty repentance, and to put your whole trust in the merits of a crucified Saviour. You know that St. Paul declares that Christ died for him, acknowledging himself, at the same time, to be the *chief of sinners.* Doubt not, therefore, that your sins are to be expiated by the means to which I have just directed you. It is the peculiar glory of God's mercy, revealed to us in His Gospel, that it is revealed specially for the benefit of sinners ; and herein we have a clear evidence that (so to speak) the greater the enormity of our sins, the greater glory do we give to God by an unfeigned exercise of Faith and Repentance. This is no encouragement to sinners, so long as they remain in their sins ; but it is all encouragement to the penitent, and, believe me, godly sorrow leads to salvation.''

The effect of this assurance, cheering as it was to me, was displayed in the clearing brow and smile of hope which betoken the rising of *the Sun of Righteousness* ; and, taking advantage of this current in our favour, I read aloud, after having begged of him to join mentally and spiritually in the exercise, the 103d Psalm.

" Yes ;" said he, after a struggle of feeling which brought forcibly to mind the conflict of Satanic agency with the spirit of holiness—" Yes ; God is above the devil."

" He is not only infinitely higher in power and glory, but He is ever ready to give this superiority to every soul which comes to Him for help—' Lord, I believe, help thou mine unbelief'—Lord, I am purposed to do thy will, oh ! give me strength to triumph over the world, the flesh, and the devil. Let this, and such, be your petitions to Almighty God ; and, be sure, He will never leave you in the power of the enemy."

In this manner we progressed through the clouds of doubt and misgiving ; and it was a happiness to see this poor returning prodigal gathering strength and confidence as he perceived those faint glimmerings of light, to which he had hitherto lived in a strange enmity, and which now bespoke a far better kingdom than the dominion of those vile elements to which he had hitherto been led captive.

" Do not," said I, in conclusion, " let any consideration rob you of your trust in the sure mercies of God. Confide in Him, fly to Him ; you are his child ; and no sooner will He suffer you, from any backwardness on His part, to be eternally lost, than you can imagine the best of fathers willing to sacrifice the best interests of his own offspring. Farewell! and may the God of all mercy, Jesus Christ our Saviour, be with you, to your comfort, now and for ever."

Thus saying, I pressed his fevered hand, and was, in a few moments, receiving the congratulations of the party of women below, one of whom offered to be the companion of my way back to the village.

This good gossip revealed to me a short account of the past life of our common friend. He had been always a notoriously dissolute character, given to fits of ungovernable anger, and was reputed, above all, to have been guilty of a crime at the very mention of which the heart shudders, and for which he lay at the mercy of an individual for preservation against the extreme penalty of the law. This last intelligence, converting my pastoral visits to the most melancholy realization of the duties of a gaol-chaplain—a change which, though on one side it seemed to elevate me to the most awful point of the office of announcing him who continually stands *between the living and the dead,* induced me to resolve on continued and increasing efforts to awaken the criminal to a thorough conviction of the efficacy of the Christian's atonement.—This intelligence I received with outward indifference, and, recommending my informant to be cautious how she gave heed to a rumour which had, probably, no foundation in truth, and, never, for her own sake, to communicate her suspicions, left her at the turn-stile which led me across the church-yard, to my own residence.

My visits, now almost daily renewed, grew more and more satisfactory. The awful burthen which oppressed his soul was at length disclosed to me; and, in an ecstacy of self-condemning gratitude, " Can there," exclaimed the convert, " be mercy and forgiveness for such a sinner as I am ?"

" My friend," said I, taking his hand, " behold, in your case, the wretched proof of that truth which is declared in Scripture that ' the devil, as a roaring lion, continually walketh about, seeking whom he may devour.' You have, indeed, been taken captive at his will; and one more fold of his accursed chain might have bound you for ever. But, thanks be to God! there is plenteous redemption; and with Him, in the exercise of His mercy to repentant sinners, *there is no respect of persons.* Your crime is not greater than mine. We have all revolted from our duty to God; and, though in our common fall, you have been precipitated to a depth from which no human aid could ever release you, your Almighty Father, who, by His word called darkness into light, *can* and *will* deliver you."

Exhortations to repentance, founded on the common topics of Scripture, were now answered by a steady and more enduring purpose of soul. Tears succeeded to and relieved the conscience of its terrors. The man grew gradually better in health; and, to my unspeakable joy, tidings were received that the unhappy partner of his guilt was lost in his passage out to some foreign settlement. This seemed to complete our work; and, when I left the parish, I had the consolation to believe that poor Mr.—— was likely to redeem the past by many years of usefulness and respectability. I wrote him an affectionate letter, which I begged he would keep as the memento of his hearty professions and resolves; and have, from time to time, heard of his continued health and apparent steadfastness.

CHAPTER XIII.

Chance is but a mere name, and really nothing in itself; a conception of our minds, and only a compendious way of speaking, whereby we would express, that such effects as are commonly attributed to chance, were verily produced by their true and proper causes, but without their design to produce them.

BENTLEY.

BEFORE I quit the short-lived honours of the Rectory, let me observe, that latterly I was not confined to the little sphere of the village congregation. I had been asked to preach in the parish church of the nearest market-town, where I had the privilege of gaining so many friends that, at the instigation of his flock, Dr. ——, the vicar, pressed me to accept the curacy, while they undertook to contribute an additional sum to the stipend. But I would not—I was, indeed, ready to do the work; but I feared that the engagements of a large parish, of between fifteen and twenty thousand inhabitants, would check that progress in reading of which I felt myself much in want; and I, therefore, gave the preference to another offer, just about the time of the expiration of my present tenure, and became the assistant-curate of a small village in the same county.

The terms were advantageous—eighty pounds per annum; the rector took all the occasional duty of the week; but, owing to his deficiency of bodily strength, the double duty of the sabbath was understood to be mine.

I had no house, nor could I obtain one within some miles; so that I settled for some months very happily in a farm-house, and was ever saved from ennui by the variety, in both sound and substance, of the almost numberless tenants of the farm-yard. I was in love; I, therefore, sat much at home, walked in green lanes at the eventide, wrote and read to the astonishment and uneasiness of my landlady, and found more real happiness, being out of the world, than any one can find in it.

It was from this less-assuming retreat that I ventured forth to pay in person those addresses in which I had never ceased to be engaged through the medium of the post-office; and, with a light purse and lighter heart, the rising lark carolled me a *God-speed* as I rode my landlord's pony to join the mail-coach, by which I sought the presence of Sarah. Nor was I slow in concluding that, inasmuch as I had a permanent office—was, in fact, the licensed curate of ————, with fourscore pounds a-year, and was, moreover, now in the full orders of a priest, my pretensions to the hand of a city broker's daughter would be not gainsayingly received.

But, alas!—the money. I had not that talisman which unlocks the hearts of men, and makes them yea or nay to all proposals. Vainly I stated the many advantages which would spring from a matrimonial connection—that " pupils " would be " received," or that my own income, slender though it was, added to what I had a right (I did not use this word) to expect with a wife, would suffice in the anticipation of better days. They were " but too happy " to receive me as their daughter's *admirer*; " but, as to marriage, really, Mr. ————, that consideration must be deferred until you possess something of a more independent nature. We have every respect for you; but, you will readily allow that we must treasure, in prospect, the happiness of a daughter."

My object, however, was to *marry*. Without influence or patronage, I never indulged myself in the contemplation of a *benefice;* but knowing my readiness, and believing my ability, to undertake that only legitimate way of eking out a curate's income, I deemed the connubial state indispensable to its success, and Hymen seemed to present the *tree of knowledge*, by which *hic, hæc, hoc* was to be inflicted on *the young idea.* The lady seemed willing to sink or swim ; but she seemed determined to consult her parents' ill-favoured *veto ;* and, had any thing of a trip before marriage entered my mind, she would have been the first to cry *stop thief!* so that, after some days of dilly-dally intercourse, I was beginning to feel myself at liberty to revoke all former decrees (for they had all explicit reference to the perpetration of wedlock), and declare myself, for the third time, *Cælebs in search,* when an event occurred—an event, in all the meaning of the word, to which something more than chance conducted.

The time appointed for my return into the country had arrived : with an air of prophetic importance, I had whispered over the inclosed hand of Sarah—" If we never meet again, farewell!" and I was now, with all the velocity of an opposition-coach, on my way from the great city to the little village—from the theatre of cracking, dashing, smashing, and uproar, to the quiet scene of cackling of geese on the distant common, the whetting of the mower's early scythe, or the monotony of the thrasher's flail. But, was there not a pleasure in the anticipation of these sounds? Ah! did ever he, who knows the beauty of the green fields, leave the whirl of town without a thrill of gentler joy, which the crack of Jehu's whip, or the more than music of the guard's tin trumpet has no power to interrupt? Well—but, the *event*.

Among my outside companions, there was one who engrossed almost all that attention which one commonly pays to the whole *melange* of associates so uninterestingly united. He was a man of countrified, but not boorish, appearance; and when he spoke, which was but seldom, it was with that strong Scotch accent and propriety of expression which may be observed in the better classes of North Britain. He was on the same seat with me, and ever and anon we found ourselves exchanging those hurried glances which bespeak the uncertain assurance of former acquaintance. " Pardon me," said I, as we entered the dining-room—" it seems that you and I have met before."—" And well met now, sir, any how," was the reply, accompanied with that rubbing of hands which betokens no lingering appetite. " We once drank o' the mountain-dew thegither; we'll now tak' a wee bit o' the roast beef of auld England."

At once reminded of the scene in Rob Roy's cave, I beheld the tempter and the deliverer—who played his part so well in the Loch Lomond expedition. I regarded the circumstance of this meeting with one, whose presence called up scenes of days gone by, as an every-day occurrence, and thankful for this solution of my wonderment, was prepared to think little more about him. But not so he: taking a seat next me, he observed, as the operations in which we were all engaged gave power of utterance, that he had much more reason to claim my acquaintance than I could be supposed capable of allowing. His manner of speech, though at first he threw in a dash of the provincial, was not, except in emphasis and enunciation, so different from my own, as to warrant any attempt at a characteristic dialogue; and my kind reader will, therefore, be pleased to receive the account of what passed between us, after our re-elevation to the coach-top—where I managed, mainly through the facetiousness of a fellow-traveller, so as to have the seat next to my old acquaintance—with as little regard to the national peculiarities of language as is convenient to a writer not possessing the versatility of a *Scott*.

All men have travelled *on* coaches—at least, all men, perhaps, whose experience of life fits them for the exercise of the *mens divinior*. There are, it is true, certain invalids, nobles and fine gentlemen, who dispise and have always been able to reject the vulgarity of riding through the liquid air *sub cælo*, side-by-side with a private soldier or a groom; but the writer of these pages is not of the *calibre* of any one of them. He has always preferred the external independence, to the internal glory of a *tête-à-tête* with my lady's maid or my lord's butler; and, on this occasion, his *fortunate* propensity gained him a deeply interesting chat with the worthy but unfortunate Highlander.

" We were taken sadly aback, my friend, in that cave; and many a time, I assure you, have I recalled to mind your services with a lively sense of their value."

" The deevil a bit o' that, sir. I did no more than any man, that is a man, and a man's a man for a' that, as the song goes, was bound to do. I took you thither, and it was my duty to see you safe back again."

" But, tell me, did you ever see my friend again? for I left him somewhat hastily."

" Friend, indeed!—and ye may ca' him that. I have listened for hours to his recitals, and have seen the tears trickle down his lank cheeks, like a bairn, when he recounted scenes, and the like, in which ye both had a hand; and may be, now he is a miserable man, and just for the sake of you and friendship."

" Then you saw him often, during the remainder of his stay?"

" I did, sir; and as often gloried in the happiness.

It was an interesting figure that ye cut, when ye presented yourselves, drippin' wet, at my own poor father's door."

" You now amaze me, sir. Pray be more explicit."

" And did Mr. B—— never tell you that the *smuggling whiskey-spinner* was the son of poor old Archy C——ll ?"

" What! and the brother of——."

His affirmative to this, like a lighted match, touched a train which led to such an explosion in my mind, that many minutes transpired before we broke silence. A length he recommenced :—

" It may be, sir, that you are much perplexed, and find it difficult to reconcile conflicting circumstances. When I first saw you I was myself a wanderer. My father's affairs had not prospered, and pecuniary responsibilities rendered it prudent for me to leave home, even in his hour of sickness. I never saw him again. On that very day, and just, I reckon, when you were appointed to the sacred office, his quiet soul went, like a weaned child, to the Almighty Parent of us all."

When I had regained sufficient composure, and perceived him restored to the self-possession which had been, as the motion of his hands within his cloak indicated, surprised by his own eloquence, I could not refrain from an endeavour to elicit from him every thing which pertained to his sister and his knowledge of B——. He, with a frankness which won my very soul, acknowledged that he had been made acquainted nearly from the first, with my addresses to Ellen, and with the manner in which they had been broken off. " But, sir," said he, " though her brother is your informant, she will never sacrifice her first attachment at the shrine of self-interest; but, like a faithful Vestal, she will die with the unquenched fire on the altar of her heart."

" Again, I do not understand you. I have, indeed, in a confused grasp, the knowledge of all you would impart; but tell me, sir; is it I who occupy that elevated seat in the affections of Miss C——ll ?"

" You are he."

" And, though I have withdrawn my pretensions?" He nodded.

" Then, boldly I ask one thing—tell it me, or not, as you please—had I ever a rival aspirant to your sister's love ?"

" You had, and he was your friend—he never knew of your attachment."

" Were you in Edinburgh about the middle of the month of October?"

" Yes; when your letter came—we were settling my late father's affairs."

" How did my letter come?"

" It was delivered by the hand of some unknown person, who, having given it in, was out of sight in a moment."

" And B—— has written since then," said I musingly to myself. " No, he has not; and I have wondered at his silence."

" The very day," he remarked, suddenly, and after a long pause which I had often but vainly attempted to break, " the very day after that letter came, came the last which we have ever heard of Mr. B——."

" How the last? Pray forgive my impatience—"

" It was a note, saying that, though he had just been made acquainted with our being in town, circumstances forbade him to take advantage of it; and, moreover, that, asking pardon for any uneasiness that might have arisen from him or on his account, he took a final leave of us for ever."

Strange indeed, as this *eclaircissement* was, I was far from being so much moved by it, or even by the contemplation of B——'s generous conduct, under circumstances of a trying nature (for, now I called to mind the fervent expressions by which he ever alluded to Ellen in conversation, and gave to them a foundation in feeling no less hallowed than my own,) as I was actuated only by another train of tumultuous thoughts.

" This coach," said I to my friend, after a pause

which had been sufficiently long to allow him to ter-
minate, on the back of the coachman—who was by
no means in love with such sentimental gentlemen,
and, therefore, rather bearishly huffed at the liberty,
two or three profound bows—" this coach, however
favourable to your *siesta*, is not, I apprehend, to be
your place of rest for the night?"

" No—about twenty miles further, I imagine, and
we part.   I shall sleep at ——, and then, on the next
lawful day, resume my journey northward."

" But, will you not spend the Sabbath with me ?
Ten miles more, and I shall be at home."

" With all my heart."

" With all my heart, I thank you," was the emphatic rejoinder I made, as I sank into a reverie from
which I was fairly aroused only by the happy moment
—so long and so painfully deferred at the latter end
of a long and cold journey—of arriving at the inn
where we alighted in order to cross the fields to my
lodging—henceforth the abode of a thousand specu-
lative charms.

" Nothing could have been more singular than our
meeting," observed he, as we stumbled over the in-
equalities of a ploughed field, with feet which had
hardly recovered their native nimbleness.

" And nothing more welcome."

Our walk was soon over.   We turned gaily into

the little village. The smiles of Saturday night peeped forth from each cottage door. The watch-dog announced our approach, and, in a moment after, sagacious " Fury" was fawning at my feet, and my honest-faced landlady, with a flaring candle in one hand, was ready, with the door in the other, to receive me.

Who knows not the calm delights of the Farm-house-parlour? The *simplex munditiis,* perhaps, has not a much better *periphrasis* than they afford. The fire, having been continually looked to by the " house"-inhabiting lady just mentioned, was the *acme* of cheerfulness—the armed-chair placed on its proper side—the candles with taper ready laid, if, indeed, the brilliance of the fire were not light enough —to crown all, the boot-jack, and slippers, all warm upon a rug of lists, are allurements worth a crown ; and the man needs not be envied who cannot be happy to his heart's content without the gewgaws of a more polished life.

Again, who knows not the real luxury of rest, refreshment, and warmth, after a hundred miles' ride? Who ever hesitated, when the question " *Tea or supper?*" was proposed, to answer " *both.*" We would the *supper,* but could not forego the *tea:* and, as by magic, another leaf was raised (the foot of flesh the while drawing out the foot of wood), and shining *casters* placed thereon. Immediately, melodious hissing was heard in the distance, the sharpening voice of the mistress urging the more than willing movements of the maid, and indications louder and louder of *des œuves et du lard,* preparing us for what, in addition to cold meat, was deemed essential to our comfort.

Once more, who knows not the *calm* and *real* delights of eating when hungry and drinking when thirsty! Some persons, indeed, affect to think it beneath the dignity of an intellectual being, to enjoy the animal satisfaction of these delights. For my own part, his intellect may be very capacious, who thus adds to his understanding the knowledge of his self-deceit; but give me a heart—yes, and a *soul*—so thankful for the supply of those things which are given us for the body that he cannot conceal the ebullitions of his gratitude even from himself.

It will be concluded that much and deeply interesting conversation was kept up till bed time. My guest informed me more fully of his father's and his own affairs—that a *murrain* carried off his black cattle—that his flocks were thinned by the *rot*—and, to complete his losses, that a rascally salesman had embezzled a large sum of money. To endeavour to obtain tidings of this delinquent had been the object of his late visit to London; but, from all that had

been made out, the fellow appeared to have embarked for Australia. The affairs of his late father,
he told me, were now happily settled, and, while contentment was the happiness of his bereaved mother
and her daughter—alas! he had not heard that they
were now orphans in the last degree; and that he
was the only prop of their ruined house—poverty,
stern poverty, was their lot. He, however, had
cheering prospects, for he was active, well-informed,
and not without many and influential friends. But,
no sooner was he committed to the all-healing hand
of sleep, than, with *a good night to all!* I betook
myself to my desk, and the following lines will sufficiently show in what manner, and to what purpose,
this eventful day was closed by me.

" Who, that lives, can say his own is not an age of
wonders? Your brother is, at this moment, my
guest. As he expects to deliver this in person,
learn from him the singular circumstances in the
midst of which we are the inmates of one house.
But, Ellen, let it be my office to claim again that
hand which stern necessity (or, rather, some wily
dæmon taking to himself this name) made me mad
enough to resign—let me atone for the slight put
upon the perfection of human loveliness and the uneasiness caused to you, by sufferings a hundred fold,
only receive me again to that sacred place in your

affections which once hallowed—nay, does now hallow every thought of my heart.

"I have learned the world already, and found it worthless—in every light but that of a necessary evil. It is an officious servant, without which, indeed, we cannot live, though its overbearing insolence, or its whining hypocrisy, is ever aiming at the mastery over us. I have learned that one pure thought—one holy love—is worth more than all it has to give; and that

> 'I have not got a world to lose,
> But would not lose thee for a world.'

"How this reminds me of the time when (and you little thought I overheard you) these words were sung by you—and I heard you—and my letter will be there too—and not I! Pardon, pardon;—but my feelings are in such a whirl that I cannot better express myself than in imploring you, as you once believed me, so to believe me now, immutably and eternally

"Yours."

CHAPTER XIV.

What is your quarrel? how began it first?
—— No quarrel, but a sweet contention.

SHAKSPEARE.

THE following morning found my friend and me pursuing our way to the little parish church.   There is a *much-ado-about-nothing* sort of bustle in the preliminaries with which a *young* clergyman occupies the early morning of the Sabbath; for he considers the *public* discharge of duty, if not almost the only, certainly by far the most momentous and all-engrossing business of his life.   But after-life sobers down this (we cannot call it unseasonable) fervour; and, gaining little by the loss of this feeling, he comes by degrees to find the cares of the world, or the concerns of his parish—the vexation of his tithes or the rancour of the dissenters about him—if he be poor, he finds the continual attempts to impose upon him by making him " pay like a gentleman,"—if easy in circumstances, he may find mortifications enough—if rich, he is in danger of finding self-importance enough, to reduce this youthful zeal, and substitute for it a business-like attention.

With me, however, at this time, all things were smooth. There were dissenters, and they none of the most amicable, in the parish; but I was not moved even by their unprovoked enmity and harmless calumny. They said, I believe, I preached *neither law nor gospel;* and one of them, a young lady to wit, once came to the church in order to have the opportunity of showing her contempt of me by going out of it as soon as she saw that I was about to preach, and then bribed the *clerk* to make a report of her conduct to the *rector.*

The public duties of the day were over, the Scotsman had occupied the chair in which I placed him last night, and soon the evening-glow of firelight blended cheeringly with the departing day. Our conversation was turning upon the public ministrations in which I had been engaged, and my friend, who was by this time found to be a zealous adherent to the *kirk,* and, having been educated at the Glasgow University, an able expositor of the peculiarities of those who follow John Knox, was liberal enough to say that I had " a zeal of God according to knowledge," and that the devotions of our congregation were at least equal to those of the Scotch Church. I remarked upon the striking contrariety of forms by which they seemed to differ from us, standing, or, rather, lolling in prayer, sitting when singing; which he parried with an observation that, in those portions of *our* service assigned to *the people*, the *clerk* was the only one who engaged, and he so *officially* as rather to diminish the little devotion which appeared to exist. "True," said I, "unhappily true—but, where is the fault? Surely not with the institution—not with the clergy; but with the people. If the few dissenters, who are actuated by any better feelings than those of political or party zeal, (having, of course, no difference of faith—such as the *professed* followers of Wesley, and all the numerous divarications of *methodism*,) would remain with us, worshipping God, according to our ritual, with that zeal which they carry to their conventicles, much of this evil (and it is an evil) would be remedied: but—let them be sober—let our sacred *things be done decently and in order*—let us have no clamouring out ' *Amen! amen!*' as if our petitions were addressed to one who loved the adoration of the lips, and such a God, in fact, as Elijah conjectured Baal to be."

I was in the course of such observations, when the door was opened (the gentle tap not having been noticed), and in stepped my friend, the Independent minister (as he was called), and the good neighbour (as I found him). This did not materially divert the intercourse, which soon received an additional voice; though I must admit, the word *dissenter* was not again used by me with that ease in which I addressed myself to a member of an established national church. I had always had a horror of any thing like *vivâ-voce* religious controversy, and studiously abstained, with my neighbour, from the mention of any word which might appear to challenge an argumentation. He was not the minister of the party above-mentioned, (they were " *Baptists*"), but of a neighbouring congregation in a populous town, and was, perhaps, for this reason, a man of some learning. My two friends, however, were not so fortunate as (or perhaps they were fortunate enough not) to steer clear of a debate; while I sat back, in something like *otium cum dig* the tacit umpire of the combat.

Such was the tact displayed by both *Presbyterian* and *Independent*, that a considerable portion of the argument remains, nearly word for word, in my memory; and, therefore, with the help of a little arrangement, here it is.

P. You deny, sir, the scripture authority of *general assemblies, kirk-sessions, synods,* and *presbyteries,* as you say we call them; but have we not here, in the fifteenth chapter of the Acts, a clear proof of the necessity of appeal in cases of doubt or contention, and of what you call interference on the part of one congregation over another? Here is an application of *the church at Antioch* to what has been called *the council of Jerusalem*—a reference from an inferior to a superior court.

I. And you endeavour, sir, to extend the authority of this example to sanction Presbyterian assemblies of every kind? but, is there no fallacy in considering an example as extending its authority, not merely to all similar cases, but to things of a quite different species?

- P. Then, you make no difference between *positive precepts of scripture*, and *scriptural examples for the authority of modern practice?*

I. A single *example* will, indeed, extend its authority to an infinite number of *similar* cases; but—

P. Nay, that is the effect of a *positive precept*. But I interrupt you—

I. —but a single example can never affect things that are no way related. When we speak of the different extent of example and its authority, we mean, if we reason justly, its extent as to different cases coming under the same head, not as to different kinds. An example has, indeed, authority beyond the particular case exhibited, and not only may, but must, include every other similar case. If the incestuous person was put away from the church at Corinth, so must every other incorrigible transgressor be put away.

P. That is exactly my argument. But, from the manner in which you treat my example of church government, I was prepared to hear you say that *only all other incestuous persons* must be put away. Surely, the crimes, murder, adultery, fraud, perjury, are of different kinds; and you said, this moment, that the *extent* of a *scriptural example*, was to be estimated, *not as to different kinds.*

I. I admit that, if the fifteenth of Acts exhibits a model of reference as to the particular case of the doctrine of circumcision, it establishes reference in general. One case being referred to any particular assembly, will prove that any other case may be referred to the same assembly; and could it be proved that this was designed as a model to fallible assemblies, it will give the authority of arbitration to that assembly which is formed upon the model here exhibited.

P. But, surely you will admit that there is no such thing on earth as *infallibility.* How, then, will you confine the operations of the Church of 1836 to the rule adopted by it when in infancy; or how can *fallible* men be restrained within bounds unnatural—

and not only so, but inaccessible to them—bounds which an *infallible* council prescribed for itself?

I. One case of reference given as an example to the churches of Christ, will prove that every doctrine, precept, and institution of the gospel, may be equally referred. But, is it accurate to say, that this reference was from an inferior to a superior *court*? Was it referred to Jerusalem by a *court* at Antioch? Was it referred by the congregation at Antioch, or any individual among them, from the decision of a court of Antioch? If neither of these can be shown to have been the case, is it consistent with truth or candour, to represent this as authority of reference *from one court to another*?

P. By such a mode of reasoning you might argue down the whole Christian Church. If you will keep out of sight, not only the altered, but also the vastly increased, circumstances of the Church, you must have but the same number of ministers—you must resort to the same places of worship—you must, in short, do everything, and no more, which was done in the age of the Apostles. I do again maintain, that the example of one council, with one case referred to it, is sufficient authority for the existence of a national Church, with proper rulers and her own peculiar legislature in matters ecclesiastical.

I. Then you forsake the guidance of Scripture?

P. By no means. The materials are retained; the form and fashion of the structure cannot, through the lapse of ages, have remained the same. The example, in the case before us, could go no further, from the nature of the case—the council was composed of inspired Apostles, and there could be no appeal from their decision. But its *authority* goes far beyond it. It is quite sufficient to authorize an appeal, or a complaint (as well as a reference) from an inferior court to a superior, and every other jurisdiction of the superior which the circumstances require. Until the Church can be shown to have the advantage of infallible rulers, this is the natural consequence of an enlarged empire deprived of actual infallibility—deprived of the power of miracles to show the reality of inspiration—deprived of such men as Peter and Paul; and having, in exchange for these, a much more—a nearly infinitely more—extensive, and a firmer hold upon the affections of mankind.

I. Had you said that, from the nature of the case, we have only one example, and, therefore, it is absurd to look for a particular example for every case to be referred, you would have reasoned incontrovertibly. But, sir, my dear sir, your reasoning is akin to this—The meetings of the primitive churches on the day on which Christ rose from the dead prove the change of the Sabbath from the seventh to the first day of the week. The example could go no further, from the nature of the case. But its authority goes far beyond it. It is quite sufficient to prove, that we should keep every day in the week as a Sabbath, as well as—

P. Nay, nay: hold, my good sir, I think you are doing my argument injustice. Here is an ordinance, from the very nature of it, fixed, invariable, and beyond the possibility of being enlarged from *one day in seven* to *the whole seven*. You might have said *any* day; and then I answer that, as on any day Christ might have risen from the dead, so on any day we might have kept the Sabbath. Did you mean *any* when you said *every*? If so, I beg pardon.

I. You said, I think, that the example of the church of Antioch authorized an appeal, complaint or reference from an inferior court to a superior, and every other jurisdiction of the superior—

P. As the circumstances of the Church of Christ, in different situations, render expedient.

I. But if the matter was here finally decided by the first court applied to, there is no room left for either inferior or superior courts—

P. There *would not be*, if we had yet an infallible council to appeal to—

I. If this assembly at Jerusalem were a presbytery,

it cuts off synods, and all superior councils on the one hand, and kirk-sessions on the other—

P. Pardon me, sir; but, since you dwell so much on names, have you no argument in favour of adopting, in all church matters, the vocabulary of the Apostles?

I. If it were a general council, nothing can be determined by any court below a general council, even in the first instance. Had this been a general council, and Presbytery of divine institution, the example here given would have exhibited the whole series of subordinate courts. We should first have heard of the decision of the kirk-session at Antioch; then of the appeal of the Church, or some part of them, to the presbytery to which they were subject; then, if this did not satisfy them, to the synod, &c. until finally they bring the matter to this general council; of the summoning and meeting, and transactions of which we should have been informed.

P. The apostle healed, and rendered sound, a cripple, by the exercise of a word. If a minister of the Gospel were, in these days, to be charged with a departure from scriptural authority, because he might take such an one, first to the surgeon of his parish, then (not being satisfied) to the faculty of a neighbouring town, then (still dissatisfied) to the county hospital, and, lastly, to the conclave of most eminent practitioners in the metropolis; would not such a charge be thought the effect of either madness or irony? Exactly the same is the case before us; and into exactly the same solution does it fall. *Inspiration and infallibility,* though both expedient at the sowing of the seed of Christianity, are not found among the branches of the tree which has now taken root far and wide upon the face of the whole earth. It is the will and wisdom of God; and man must thankfully submit. For want of this due consideration, *Independents,* while they neglect or explain away a great part of the *practice* which is clearly founded in the Bible, *affect* to fix down the practice of modern times to the precise *letter* of the *examples* they choose to refer to, though ever so contrary to their *true spirit and design.*

I. Allow me to ask you, sir, what is that great part of the practice, clearly founded in the Bible, which Independents neglect or explain away? If you can show us this, we will be your debtors. We have no *standards,* like you, to prevent us from receiving any part of truth when discovered.

P. Our *standards,* allow me to inform you, are to prevent us, if possible, from receiving any part of error; and I conceive that the very *spirit,* so clearly indicated by your denomination, is no part of the Spirit of Truth which dictated the word of God. I am not a minister of my church; but I am quite assured that the authority for church-government is express and clear, and I believe that the form and manner of it are left, in a very great measure (always provided they be not at variance with the authority of Scripture) to the discretion of those who preside. There is a *human* part, as well as a spiritual part of the Church of Christ, and if Independents were, as they affect to do, to shake off that which is human, I fear that they, or we, (should we adopt the same conceit) would cut a very sorry figure as a church.

I. Just in the same manner, Presbyterians allege that Independents neglect some part of apostolical practice, not to induce them to comply with it, but to excuse themselves for the neglect of apostolical institutions. And pray, my good sir, what is it you mean by the opposition which you seem to suppose as existing between *the letter* of an example, and its *true spirit and meaning?* I have been in the habit of thinking that the Bible *speaks* just what it *intends,* and that its language is, in itself, the fittest of all others to convey its meaning.

P. Then, sir, allow me to ask you one question— When our Lord directed his disciples *(spiritually)* to turn the other cheek to him who had smitten the one, to give the cloak also to him who would steal the coat, and to shake off the dust from their feet, when they departed from a house or city, in which their words had been rejected; do you affirm that we ought to obey (*literally*) the directions? or, when he spake, with a *spiritual design*, of the difficulty—nay impossibility of a rich man entering into the kingdom of God, did he *literally* pronounce eternal ruin to all the possessors of wealth? But, I wish for no greater proof of the possibility of opposition between the *letter* and the *spirit*, than the apostle's declaration that

" The letter killeth, but the spirit giveth life."* We wander, however, from our first subject, and I wish to make but one more observation before (as I think we now *must)* we close our conversation. Every pin of Presbytery could not possibly be found in any scripture example; although the general system is not only explicitly, but clearly, authorized by the practice of the primitive Church *as far* as the cases occurred.

I.   The pontiff may defend his usurpation in the same language; and, in this way, we might make as many additions to the Scriptures as we pleased.

Differing from both, I was studious to avoid offering any opinion upon the subject of this controversy. Had I been asked, however, for my suffrage, I should have said, the advocate of Presbytery had the better

---

* 2 Cor. iii. 6.

of the argument; for, when we certainly find in the New-Testament-churches, three distinct denominations in the ministry, *Bishops, Presbyters, (or Priests)* and *Deacons;* we must certainly lean to the opinion that the two former were one and the same officers, much rather than that church-government is not authorized in Scripture, beyond that very inefficient and dangerous kind of it which places but one minister over each congregation which they call *a church.* I remember, in the town in which I was born, a circumstance, which created much gossip and a great deal of petty and contemptible observation, strongly illustrative of the evils which may arise from the cultivation of the spirit of *independence.* The minister of that particular sect, a young man of good address and genteel appearance, so far captivated the heart of a young lady of the flock that she took the liberty of avowing her affection to him by letter. Whether from a prior engagement, or from a vow of celibacy, or from want of reciprocity, or from what cause soever, the maiden was rejected, notwithstanding her repeated supplications. These, however, became at last so wearisome to the minister that he *told it to the church, i. e.* in one of his sermons, made a public complaint of the importunate fair one.

CHAPTER XV.

———

What fire is in mine ears? Can this be true?
  Stand I condemn'd for pride, and scorn so much?
Contempt, farewell! and maiden pride, adieu!
  No glory lives behind the back of such.
And, Benedick, love on, I will requite thee;
  Taming my wild heart to thy loving hand;
If thou dost love, my kindness shall incite thee
  To bind our loves up in a holy band:
For others say, thou dost deserve; and I
Believe it better than reportingly.
                              SHAKSPEARE.

———

MONDAY morning came and my guest departed. Other mornings were succeeding each other, when one shone out from among the rest as the harbinger of a letter from my ever valued friend, B——.

He cleared up the mystery which had always hung about my former correspondence with Ellen, by an acknowledgment that we had been unconsciously rivals;—that he had always been assured, from both what was said and what was written respecting *friendship* and *priority*, of the existence of some impediment, though never till my letter came could he conjecture what; and that, having now ascertained that his friend was the fortunate pre-occupant of the lady's attachment, he contentedly withdrew from the pursuit. Upon reflection, I could not suspect Ellen of duplicity in the entertaining of two lovers at the same time : for it was evident that her feelings were of that delicately fine and susceptible texture, that it were impossible for her to act otherwise than she had done. Her allusions to this rivalry, in letters to each, were enough to clear her of all imputations prejudicial to her integrity of heart; and the more I reflected upon all the facts brought together, the more convinced was I that, with her mind and sentiments, she pursued the only course which the circumstances permitted. *Friendship*, in her view, was a holy fellowship—more binding than *fraternity*. If, then, one member suffered, the whole body must sympathise in its suffering; and she could not bring her mind (indeed, things had not proceeded far enough to enforce an attempt to bring it) to consider the necessity of cutting off one, that the other might be unencumbered; and contenting herself with occasional enigmatic disclosures of her feeling, she left to the course of events the elucidation of the real state of the case.

But, not many days afterwards, came Ellen's letter, in reply to mine by the hand of her brother; and, as the reader may not be disinclined from a desire to know something of her feelings from herself, notwithstanding that which may be conjectured from what has been already disclosed, I shall present him with a copy.

" *There is a Providence that shapes our ends, rough hew them as we will,* is the observation of some one; and never was it more fully verified than in the singular meeting of you and my brother. I have drawn from him every word of it with an avidity which none can know—need I tell you what he says of your hospitality and of you ?

" And now, ———, what do you expect in answer to your letter ? Shall I yield to the fashion of the world, and confess that the imputation of capriciousness, laid upon my sex, is true ; or shall I obey the emotions of my heart, and unfold at once the happiness which I have derived from its few, but expressive, lines ?

" Like a stream which has been suddenly stopped in its exulting career, and now begins to overflow its banks, making for itself new channels ; I was endeavouring to submit to the decision which your candour avowed ; and (in equal candour) my feelings, by taking to themselves different currents, according to the outward circumstances of my life, might have been so far composed, in time, as to leave the remainder of my life a wretched blank. I confess to you that I was willing to acknowledge and to be guided by the hand which was evidently at work in the destinies of our poor and afflicted family; and when I had lost your affection, and the solace which it would have afforded, I entered into the melancholy satisfaction of grief. It was better to be in the house of mourning than in the house of joy.

" But now, again, my life—nay, is it not my existence?—resumes its wonted gladness. Poverty (for, ————, we are now very poor) has in it a pleasure sanctified by the disinterestedness of your affection ; and I can pursue those household occupations which now devolve upon me, with a heart which is filled with contentment, resignation, and thankfulness to Him who is, indeed, a Father of the fatherless. Now all is again a field of real, though sad, delight. I visit the gate at which (first and last) we parted, and mark the winding path which you and your *dear* companion took. I see, in imagination, your figure emerging from the hollows and ascending the intervening hills, and again decreasing over every brow— nay, (will you believe my folly ?) I take a delight in walking where you walked, and talking, as if your spirit were my companion; and there is old Stuart, that amusing old neighbour—who gives me such droll accounts of you, speaking of you, and particularly of your friend, with such delighted admiration, that I brave all the old man's *badinage*—an engine which, I fear, is not employed solely by even the guests at his house. He tells me how you insisted upon having, and what appears much more singular, paying for dinner and supper, both at one meal—how you laughed at each other in your masquerading attire, and how you enjoyed your row upon the loch in the morning. These things now make the sunny hours of my life.

" My brother has quite charmed me with the account of his sojourn with you. Alas! how good of you not to unlock the floodgates of sorrow!

" I fear you found him a *zealot*, almost a *bigot*, in religion; but, if I may venture an opinion, surely that which is solely calculated to promote the peace and happiness of mankind, ought never to be allowed to become cause of bitterness or contention. He is a dear brother, and you must pardon any thing like intemperance, which may have appeared in his zeal for the established religion of his country, for the sake of

" ELLEN C——LL."

Forthwith I contemplated matrimony. *Hymen*

stood, torch in hand, like the link-boys of olden times, ready, and even solicitous, to conduct me to his fane; but, as I did not wholly disregard those saws and maxims about imprudent and improvident matches which the older portion of mankind have off by heart, I sat down and counted my means.

Clear was it that I ought to marry—clear that I could not well support a wife upon my present income—clear that, as a clergyman, my hopes of a better were very slender. I had neither family nor influence whereby to get a church-living—though I begin to find out that I have just enough of both to exclude me from such a boon—just blood enough to be above *toadying,* just enough of influence to make ordinary men afraid of exalting me. My ideas of the bishop's munificence were completely quashed by the very significant intimation that, *being admitted into orders* (along with many others, who had certainly not done any thing — whereas I had done nothing *plus* something) was the reward of what I had done. I was not tempted, by the possession of money, to follow the example of Simon Magus. But, I was able to teach; and my ideas and habits had long been accustomed to this mode of life. I concluded, that a man willing to work would find employment; and that the married-state was a *sine quâ non* to the well-being and well-doing of the pæda-

gogue, was a conclusion to which I attained with
equal facility. So long as the people eat bread, the
honest baker will thrive; so methought, in these
universal-knowledge days, he who is willing and able
to teach will certainly find encouragement. *Bread,*
as I often reasoned with those who had some right
to canvass with me the subject of my speculations, is
necessary for the maintenance of the body ; and *education* is the food which, in these days above all, is
deemed equally indispensable to the mind ; and he
who *will* educate, one would think, should live, while
he who *can* educate, as I added with a self-assurance
of which even now I am not ashamed, *must* live.
The succession of weeks tended to mature my plans,
and to increase my confidence. A house, in a neighbouring village, was thought of, and looked at. It
was to be had *furnished.* I had no money (my jour-
neys to and from London had impoverished me);
but , then, the occupant was so desirous of changing
his quarters, that he would take my notes at six and
twelve months, in payment for the furniture. This
promised well; for in that time my success in pupilizing would enable me, with slight assistance, to
meet my engagements. Besides, my salary would
come up as a *corps de reserve.* All things, in short,
bore such a flattering aspect, and my correspondence
with Ellen so warmed and stimulated my projects

that, having resolved to act, I invited my father not only to come and talk over the matter, but actually to survey the place of intended operations, and said, with all the magnanimity (perhaps more) of the hunchback king,

> " I have set my life upon a cast,
> And I will stand the hazard of the die."

Nothing, to such a father, could be more welcome than the probability of happiness to his son. He, accordingly, sanguine as myself, entered into the good hope of success which presented itself; and we spent together a few of the most pleasant days which have fallen into the warp of a life which bids fair to be as chequered as his was. *That* life is spent: *this* runs on; and (whatever may be) not yet has arisen in its course any good reason to repent of an alliance formed in spite of all the sordid, narrow, arrogant, and self-important dogmas of the world. That trust, in the goodness of a providence which sustains and over-rules all man's little puny efforts at management and discretion, in which I entered the most sacred of all human engagements, has not yet belied me; and, more than this, it never will.

Brief let me be. Another journey to London, (for the remaining family had repaired to the neighbour-hood of the English capital) crowned me with a wife;

for " a virtuous woman is *a crown* (the rustic engravéd upon the tomb-stone 5*s*., in order to fill up the line) to her husband;" and I returned, thus wedded, to my new house, to carry into effect all the schemes, which had been so well agitated, and were already in motion, for the acquirement—of pupils, and, *par consequence,* a decent maintenance for a wife and family—the *familia* being already made up of a villanous old housekeeper, consigned to me, as a servant of all work, and an heir-loom, by the legacy of my predecessor, and a silly old man, who was a *ranter*, to look after the garden, and do the deeds beneath the dignity of an antique and portly spinster.

Who has not been at a wedding? Let him go; for it is the sure road to a week's happiness. If, however, he select a curate's wedding, the felicity may be all at his own *expense*. But, though one may not have been at such a celebration, surely any account of it would convey no new idea to the courteous reader's mind. May I not also excuse myself from entering into any detail of the events of those few preceding weeks which *etiquette,* even in our unassuming condition, demanded. There were, I believe, all those joyous and heart-thrilling flutterings common to all but the cold-blooded speculators who are united in matrimony, like the quarterings in their coats of arms, with a purse on one side, and a title on the other, or, wed themselves, for love of gold, to the wrinkles of old age. It was not so in our case. The union was one of sincerity, and all those steps which led to it were taken in simplicity and spotless affection.

One circumstance only will I mention. Being in that profession upon which, of all others, is inculcated brotherly love, I called on the vicar of the parish, signified my intention, paid the sum demanded for a licence, and received from him a promise that he would, *with pleasure,* perform the required service, on the day and at the hour appointed. This I of course received as an intimation of a kindness such as even I would not have dared to deny to a professional brother: but, no—the time came, and the fee of one pound was demanded, in the hearing of the vicar, by that useful functionary, the clerk, and paid. Thus early was I initiated into the mystery that, of all living men, the clergy are least united in themselves, and least inclined to bear one another's burdens; and that, while even lawyers shew mercy one to another, and medical men invariably afford gratuitous succours, not only to, but in aid of, their brethren, the clergy rigorously exact, one from another, every farthing of their due.* Thus, of law, physic, and divinity, the

* The truth of this has been verified in the demand of an exorbitant fee for the interment of my father when I was the only

last alone is inexorable; and thus do I conclude this chapter with an assertion, the truth of which accounts, more, perhaps, than any other single cause, for the hostility and defection on the part of the people towards the establishment — not altogether directly, indeed, but indirectly, in such a manner as I hope hereafter to show to the satisfaction (sorry as such a satisfaction must be), of every candid friend of the church. Every man is a player on the stage of life; and, if one would make the audience weep, he must shed tears—if he would have them kind, considerate, warm-hearted, compassionate; let *him* first be tender —be pitiful—be courteous.

mourner. Also, recently, when I begged permission of a London Rector to baptize six children of a friend in his church, permission was granted, but the *fees* were sent for.

CHAPTER XVI.

A discreet learned clergyman, with a competency
fit for one of his education, may be an entertaining,
an useful, and sometimes a necessary companion.

SWIFT.

My next communication from B—— was of a nature
somewhat unexpected, though one which was calculated to afford me real pleasure—*i. e.* if one can
really rejoice in the welfare of another.   An uncle of
his, the incumbent of a rectory on the eastern coast,
had somewhat suddenly paid the last debt which we
all owe to the laws of that frail nature under which we
live, and the preferment was offered by his grandfather
to B——.   It was, of course, accepted; for B——
was a *marrying* man, and the tenure of his fellowship
imposed on him a restriction which circumstances
alone had compelled him to observe.   Term-time had

arrived, and he was now reading for orders and domiciled in his old rooms at Cambridge.

Well, thought I, for once this monkish ordinance is foiled in its purposes—one man, at least, is not obliged, in order to retain the means of living, to run counter to the law which God and nature sanction; and B—— has too much generosity in his nature not at once, now the necessity of retaining them no longer remains, to throw off the shackles of celibacy—he will resign his fellowship and marry—or, rather, he will marry, and, after a year of *grace*, make way for some one who has long indulged the pious hope that he would soon either *marry* or *go to heaven*.

The writer of these pages would hardly agree that fellows of Colleges might marry and retain their fellowships; but, what would go far towards bringing into effect all the advantages which are vainly looked for in the present system, there might, reasonably, be such a thing as holding fellowships for a certain time. At all events I see no reason why our Colleges, having thrown aside the " superfluity of naughtiness" which distinguishes the traditions of men from the commandment of their Maker, should yet retain the abomination of monastic celibacy. If we examine this question *pro* and *con.*, we must conclude, I think, that the present system is faulty, to say the least, if not, to say the most, offensive to the Divine source of all power.

The best reason which I ever heard given in favour of this anti-matrimonial regulation, is that men, thus unencumbered with the cares of life, are much more qualified for the prosecution of those studies by which science and literature are kept alive and carried on to successive stages of improvement. Is it so? Is that roving vessel, called man, more to be relied on, without an anchor, such as marriage is so well calculated to afford, for the attainment of these objects? Is he not much more likely, when his habitation is that of a citizen of the world, to effect a sure and sufficiently rapid progress in art and knowledge, than while he finds himself a being wrapped up in the selfish, torpid and unaspiring competency, which most of our college fellowships will at once bestow upon him? Not permitted, moreover, to follow the bent of inclination, men will too often give themselves to a baneful course of *attentions* without *intentions*, or of intimacies without the staying influence of virtue. Who has not known of instances in which the fellow's income is not *wholly* devoted to the maintaining of himself in credit and freedom from the wants of life? There are young fellows who cannot marry, and old fellows who will not; but, where are the fellows who cannot or

will not stoop to a substitution for that which is
" honourable in all men?" There are some, doubtless; but they are few.

But, you will say, the man, who is bent on (let us
say) disinterested wedlock, may, for a term of years
so husband his fellowship as eventually to bring it to
the same issue as if he held his preferment of necessity for such a term and not longer. He *may*, but *will*
he? Our dispositions are refractory enough; and
few would be rendered more tractable by the imposi-
tion of additional trammels. Let a man know that
so long and no longer will the sun shine, and he may
be induced to make his hay; but, under a conviction
that his opportunity is coeval with his life, he will
seldom be in a hurry, though his wishes may direct
him to the adoption of the *means* necessary to the
end : and thus, day after day—nay, year after year—
rolls on, and he begins—not to save his money,—unless, indeed, he be a niggardly *fellow* who need not be
suspected of meditating anything so generous as the
consummation of an honest attachment to " a poor
maiden."

We argue, you see, upon the assumed expediency
of a married life; and, candidly, we do abjure, as de-
testable, opposed to divine law and human advantage,
and injurious (as far as it goes) to the public morals,
a forced compliance with an unscriptural dogma

which places a restraint, both unnatural and unholy, upon our most honourable propensity. And, besides all this, if regulatious were introduced to limit the tenure of these *sinecures* (if they may be so called), a stimulus would be generated through the whole body of the rising generation in our universities, which, crowded as they are, could not fail of yielding much good. The genius would not flag, because all avenues to college-preferment are seemingly choked by the *fortunati* of a former period; nor would the talents of many a promising under-graduate be suffered to go uncultivated, because the prospect of reward is obscured by the *divine right* of those who will forfeit, only with their lives, the " pretty things," from which they have long found it impossible to part; and who, perhaps, have already contracted those emergencies which render extremely desirable the retention of all their " means and appliances."

" You know enough of me," says B——, " to congratulate me upon an emancipation from a slavery which, while it really degrades, affects to exalt us to the proud eminence of literary *conservatism;* and I need not allude to your blissful condition in order to awaken your suspicions on the score of my disposition to follow the example."

And it is a *slavery,* as that which fetters or may fetter the free actions of an honourable man deserves to be called. We have cast off, and abjure the superstitions and follies of Popery; and yet, strange as it appears, in our very seats of useful and religious learning we preserve the most loathsome scab of the leprosy.

Well, according to all this, B——'s marriage was duly announced in the course of the following spring; and he entered upon the duties of his pastoral office. We still corresponded—a fact not a little surprising, when it is considered that two friends both marry and yet continue friends; and which can only be accounted for by the assistance of another fact—he married my wife's sister. As " there is a tide in the affairs of *men*," so is there a time in which *women* ought to make or mar their fortunes ; and, simply because she was a prize for any man, Julia was not one of those young ladies who think themselves sure of getting off and therefore trifle with every offer. But it was odd that, after having paid some *devoirs* to the elder, he should wheel off to the younger of the two sisters. Nevertheless, his determination was a good one.

It would be very impertinent in me to talk of the honey-moon of my friend B——, when I have my own to attend to. Not even did we pay them a visit; and, therefore, all I could say would be hazarded upon conjecture. B—— was soon settled in a de-

lightful parsonage. Summer suns clothed the neighbouring sea in every attraction, while the summer
foliage wrapped up their calm retreat in a security
which seemed to defy every unwelcome attendant on
old Ocean. His church, perched up upon a head-
land, was a favourite beacon among sailors; and
many were the legendary tales which the young
reefer drank in during the midnight watch from the
eloquent lips of some old tar. " There, your honour,
many's the time as me and poor old Tim Bowling ha'
seen in that there church-yard, and up o' th' roof on't,
afore a 'saster at sea, long trains o' mourners following
after coffins hung about wi' long black—what d'ye
call 'em? (Palls, I suppose)—you're right, your
honour. Well, mony's the time, at midnight, as
we've seen 'em walk about, wi' burnin' tapers in their
hands and in white garments, just when a Nor'
Easter's been sending us down, wi' bare poles, fifteen
knots an hour." And even the middies' mess—nay
the captain's cabin-dinner—was enlivened, or dead-
ened, with less appalling tales of " how often that
little church has been the receptacle of the wrecked
and drowned, and the cold flags of its modest chancel
been bespread with lifeless bodies of brave fellows
washed on shore, or dashed, while struggling for it,
on the hard and unfeeling rocks."

" Our church-yard," says B——, " tells a sad

tale ; and many an evening—now that the sea would tempt the most timorous to her bosom—do parties resort to it to muse upon the many sentiments which recal the virtues and the hardships of those who sleep beneath."

"One monument, raised by my predecessor, records the fate of a gallant boat's-crew, who perished in their attempt to reach the hull of a transport not half a mile from shore. Another, commemorative of the fate of a young French officer, who was found expiring on the very spot where his body now rests, from the combined effects of exhaustion and the contusions which were inflicted before he was thrown high enough by the surge to escape the devouring wave which succeeded, bears this inscription :—

'By foreign hands my dying eyes were clos'd—
By foreign hands my mangled limbs compos'd.'

He whispered ' Marianne,' and, with his eyes raised up to heaven, emitted his last breath in a deep ' Adieu !'"

But the part of my friend's correspondence, which most interested me, was that in which he replied to my remarks upon the inadequacy of a Curate's means to the work which, in order to maintain universal respect, he must do.

"I do, indeed," says he, "enter most entirely into

your complaints; and something ought to be done to render the estate of every clergyman one of competence. I, on the contrary, possessing the means of relieving their wants, am (I am sorry to say) not only nearly worshipped by the poor, but also lauded by the middling class of farmers, and respected by the *great*—you know what I mean by this word. There is not a dissenter in the parish; here, happily, there is no division—no revolt—no mock-institutions. I am their accepted pastor, and, as far as I know how, (and Julia helps me,) I do my duty among them: they are my flock, and they cheerfully follow my directions. It seems as if it *would be* a crime with *them* to depart from the worship of their fathers; and, though there are, of course, some moral delinquents who, now and then, go astray; yet, I will venture to affirm that we have not, in a population of five hundred and thirty, one person who would wrong, go beyond, or defraud, his brother in any thing. No, ——, we have no whining hypocrites, and consequently, we have no cheats and rogues amongst us. What is the state of things with you, where you have as many sects as there are days in the week, I can very well imagine; for I never found an extraordinary profession of religious principles (and nearly every species of dissent, I believe, involves this) without a correspondent addiction to fraud and dishonesty, or indulgence in known and forbidden sin. You must not, however, suffer these trials to wean you from the remembrance of the glorious commission which we bear, to follow our great master in all things; and I can almost make myself believe, that, in appointing you to a vineyard so choked up with briers and thorns, and so wasted by the wild boar of the forest, the Almighty Disposer of all things has a special providence in behalf of your future usefulness in His church. Nothing, you know, can be too great a service—Oh! where shall we find one acceptable? —to him who hath laid down his life for his friends."

This advice was good—it was excellent: so was the fountain from which it came. But B—— had rather mistaken me. He thought I was annoyed, personally, by those things which the reader will be acquainted with in the sequel: and nothing is more common than to distort that indignation—may I say, *righteous* indignation?—which one feels on account of the frightful wickedness and deceit of mankind, into a morbid fretfulness. They who torment your soul with their abominations, think they mortify and insult *you;* and while they offend God by their flagrant *boast* that they *can do mischief,* they aggravate their guilt by attributing the wrath of the Maker to one of the creatures made.

Poverty has its evils: but these *all* come to those who, obliged to maintain an appearance of comfort, if not affluence, are subject to its rule. Trifling losses, for instance, which are the effects of accident or mischief, will often disturb the peace of a poor family; and those conflicting anxieties, which all the members of it mutually feel, if they have any feeling, will often tend to quarrels and disagreements, not only painful to those concerned but giving occasion of scandal to the busybodies in other men's matters, who abound in every rural parish. And, if this be true of all people, it is especially so of the poor clergyman's family which, out of the common insolence and overbearing of the world, is set down, almost universally, for public property—though, when they come to want assistance, we find how many really felt any proper concern for them. You cannot destroy the worship of gold in this country; the calves are set up in both Bethel and Dan; and, so long as the world lasts, the enquiry of old England will be, *Has he got any money?* Interference, with regard to the movements and pursuits of a clergyman so circumstanced, is another burden which we have to bear. Our characters being public in some respects, the good gossips insist upon publicity in all other matters; and some Dissenters have, in their generation, most wisely taken advantage of 'this; for they provide the minister's wife, as I am informed, not only with an *accoucheur* but also with a *nurse.* Oh, John !—thou art a very silly old gentleman after all.

CHAPTER XVII.

O when meet now
Such pairs in love and mutual honour join'd ?

Milton.

HONEY-MOONS are pleasant things; and not the less so because the couple concerned are generally quite in the dark as to the probability of succeeding moons being less mellifluous than their leader. Certain that no forebodings operated upon ours. It was our lot to be of that *caste* called the middle class; and, as no carking cares, nor pains of absence, consequent upon the necessity of out-door labour, on the one hand, so, on the other, no slavish submission to the thraldom of greatness, was permitted to mar the concord, which, in our cottage surrounded by its flowery garden—*love* dwelt there *among the roses*—kept perpetual holiday during the reign of at least one moon. It was a contest in which each strove " to steal the sweet and honied sentences " of the other.

My mother had received us, at the termination of a dusty journey from town, as the wheels of our chaise announced the arrival; and the little cage, adorned with *bouquets* from a garden, the attractions of which were then invisible, and tastefully lighted, seemed a fit receptacle for one whose ornaments were those which nature gave her, and who was not adorned with any of the adventitious appendages of rank or wealth.

Let it not be surmised, however, that we journeyed a hundred miles at the expensive rate of posting. No—this *eclat* was fresh from the nearest market-town; and, as we well knew how little money we could spare, the bulk of the journey was performed on the top of a stage-coach.

We were in that department which is peculiarly dependent on the courtesy and protection of the guard ; and right well did we enjoy the narrative with which this droll character beguiled the *tædium* of our wayfare. He was a fine, tall figure of a man ; and, from his gait and speech, we had every reason to believe him when he announced that he had once gloried in a commission to wear the sword of his Majesty. If we were to believe all besides, he was a *roué* of the first style, had spent more money than most honest people ever possess, had married his wife, who was a baronet's daughter, by stealth from a convent in France, or Flanders, and had embraced the avocation he now pursued in order to elude the father's stern purpose of starving them into a separation. All these things, set off in all the attractions of circumstance, were told in a manner which asked for credence, and certainly gained attention so far as to render the journey very amusing. But he was a droll character. Whether it was " Phœbus' flickering front " in his face, I know not; but he had such a singular habit of contracting the spaces allotted to his eyes, and twisting up his features, that the only description to be given of it was that he seemed as if he were continually munching unripe gooseberries. He was also droll in the observations which he soon acquired the liberty of making upon us and our fellow-travellers, and declared that we had not been married six-and-thirty hours. In this acquiesced also all the rest, and particularly one young woman who, having asked my wife secretly what I was, paid her the overwhelming compliment that she *thought* I was *something out of the common*. But enough of this brilliant introduction to the nuptial lot. The day was gloriously fine, and the country beautiful ; we went a capital pace ; and there was more variety, if our mode of travelling had not all the *splash-dash* which attends the departure of some happy couples for the country mansions of their friends. Horses we had four : and what did we suffer from the company of our fellow-travellers, motley though they were? Ha! but we did not pay the *money*— and here we are again upon the horns of that great and alarming *dilemma* which, while it very much distracts, entirely befools, the world.

My mother, as I said, *received* us; and this will convey more than could be expressed in many words to those who are at all conversant in such tear-dropping scenes of bliss. Though man is doomed to labour and sorrow, and though the earth bears the curse of his apostasy, there are some drops of honey in the cup, and they are sometimes found even unmixed with the bitter draught which our poor mother earth presents to all her children.

Well: the sun shone day after day. At home we had roses and strawberries : abroad, the rich cornfield either waved in luxuriant abundance, or presented the more animated scenes of harvest. My church was undergoing extensive repairs, and this circumstance left me at leisure to join in the ceremony of appearing at church; and that was not a small affair. But, I must approach this imposing ceremony by degrees. The morning after our arrival, with the very first dawn of a summer's day, three bells pealed forth (as well as they were able) the nuptial roundelay, and three half-crowns elicited three graceful bows from the triumvirate which presided over this performance. We were invited, moreover, to the *honour of* a tea-drinking (at our expense) on the occasion; but declined, much to the annoyance of some half-dozen rustic matrons, a compliment which they very disinterestedly declared to be the custom of the parish. But Sunday morning came, and to church we went. There were all eyes awake, down from the rector's governess to the curtsey-dropper of the aisle, and embracing all the other sex within the confines of the " merry little ploughboy that whistled o'er the lea," and the 'squire's graceless son.

The succeeding days of the week brought the rapper into more use than heretofore ; the *calls* were manifold and various ; and great was the consumption of cake and wine. The rector, his lady, the governess, and three or four of the rector's lady's friends, at once put every chair in our little drawing-room under the articles of *wear-and-tear ;* then followed, during the week, the squires and their ladies, the farmers' ladies without their lords, the nearest apothecary and his sister, and all—even all who were *gentle*, within the sound of the trumpet with which fame had heralded our entrance to the wedded state.

Then came the returning of these formalities—then, certain dinners, in which the parsonage-folks, as they had ample means, took the lead—then my mother went—then my sister came—then came slander and ill-nature—then came the damp and rainy autumn— then, winter, bringing newts into our cupboards and rheums into our frames—then came an invitation to spend Christmas at my father's house, which, especially as with all these comings there came no answers to my advertisements for pupils or clerical employment, we gladly accepted; and, in the train of this, came the first display of open hostility on the part of this naughty world.

The coach, (coach again! oh the vulgar things!) by which we intended to travel from the neighbouring county-town, set out so early in the morning that we deemed it expedient to sleep there the preceding evening; and for this purpose hired a chaise to take us thither over-night. Well pleased were we also to have got rid of our house to another medical aspirant upon terms similar to those on which I took it; and thus, with light hearts, we felt ourselves at-home in every part of the world—houseless, indeed, but rich, in having received one-half of the valuation of our goods and chattels.

But there were too many points in all this on which to hang the gloomy curtains of suspicion, to allow the good folks of this world to escape the indulgence of their favourite study—*other men's matters.* We had made a trip by moonlight, and had evidently run away—this was the charitable construction which, beginning with the low and ignorant, very soon climbed up into the heads of their betters, and not only carried away all our own friends, not excepting *my own rector* (according to common *parlance*), but also brought after us, with blood-hound dexterity, one or two emissaries from our palpitating tradesmen in the aforesaid county-town. My good father fumed, my mother looked concerned, and my wife wept; but I had even then so much philosophy, that I lifted up my voice and laughed—yea, laughed aloud, to think that a man must needs employ the public crier, or be voted to the tender mercies of the hang-man, whenever he perpetrates any movement beyond a call upon his neighbour or the daily visit to his stable. (For *stable,* in my case, read pig-sty; for horse I had none, but pigs I had two).

My father's respectability was sufficient to settle at once this *hubbub,* and to crush the opening persecution in its bud. But, though the world is ready to condemn, it seldom has grace to confess; and the spleen of the bad people seemed, though diverted from its course, increased by the disappointment. It had lost its prey, and like the worn-out fowler, for very vexation damned the object which it could not murder, and gave a blow to my poor character from which it was long before it recovered. I was not, however, disposed to yield one jot; *nullâ pallescere culpâ* was my pride; and though my rector was so far unmanned by the malice of neighbours as to give me an intimation which meant something like *a notice to quit,* I stood upon my *licence,* and firmly determined to return and brave out this puny storm, stirred up as it was by a horde of pigmies, whose thunders would have been those of cloud-propelling Jove, had I yielded to their pitiable fury. Oh world! world! how truly contemptible thou art in reality, and yet how much we love thee! How ready are thy slaves to run, like ragged street-boys, behind the wheels of him who rides in triumph, because, armed with a good conscience, he has courage to defy them! I returned; with all the indignation of insulted rank, closed my accounts with my tradesmen, telling them that had not my profession dictated nobler conduct, the horsewhip might have served them better; and had the satisfaction (for it was a satisfaction) of receiving a complete *amend* from the rector with whom I was clerically engaged, which has been followed even to this moment by a series of uninterrupted kindness and friendship; and reminded the other mentioned rector that the various services which I had done for him were to be compensated by something more current (for the time to come) than his good dinners, paid for as they were by our equally good company.

It is certainly a grovelling fallacy to suppose that, when invited to place your knees under the covering of another man's table-cloth, he is the Cr. and you the Dr. Perhaps it might more often be reversed ; for I have lived to know the value of *time* and a total indifference to this sort of *favours*. " The Stranger," in the drama, has a good sentiment on this.

We were now domiciled in the county-town aforesaid, where I paid rather more than half my annual income in rent and taxes, with a view to obtain pupils ; and at length I had *one*. More than ten miles from my cure, I walked thither and back commonly, and performed with pleasure those duties which for their earthly reward, had the wages of my Lord ——'s under-butler, about one-third of his importance in the eyes of my flock, and nearly all of it in his.

CHAPTER XVIII.

—

'Tis slander;
Whose edge is sharper than the sword, whose tongue
Outvenoms all the worms of Nile.

SHAKSPEARE.

—

IN that state of life which usually goes by the name of
confined, or limited, circumstances, few minds can
triumph over a disposition to inactivity. Sitting at
home, reading and moping are certainly the greatest
evils of poverty, and on this account, I would have
its circumstances called confining. If, however, any
disappointed young man should have his eye on this
line, let him take a word of counsel from one who can
sympathize with him. Move about—go, wherever
you can—introduce the subject of your wants; and
people are commonly so fond of talking, and news, on
this account, flows into such an infinite ramification of
streams, that you cannot fail of soon hearing of

" something to your advantage." The greatest evil
to be found from this is that, though you may not be
unfortunate enough to fall into the hands of Joseph
Ady, you will scarcely escape the claws of some
" clerical agent," anxious to serve you.

A young clergyman has certainly the privilege of
holding converse with all the curates in his neighbourhood; and these are the very men who know
most of the passing events. You will be sure to hear
of some one about to vacate his situation, or that such
a curacy is now vacant. The evils of brooding over
confining means are incalculable. Body and mind
suffer equally. The energies of both are destroyed,
the temper is soured, the dispositions perverted. The
world would recommend you to have *impudence*
enough; but we must give the same quality a better
name, and call it *confidence.* But the greatest of all
acquisitions is a gentleman-like and deferential style
of writing or speaking, if this be to be acquired—
such a man *nascitur, non fit,* some may say; but yet
much is to be done by the perseverance of Demos-
thenes. Without it, there is but little chance of rising
above the refuse—with it, you want only conduct to
ensure ultimate success: for, whether you have
splendid testimonials or otherwise, it has a certain
Aladin's-lamp-like property. If you are a *good* man,
it prevents envy and detraction; if not, it flatters your

wished-for patron into a liking for you. Almost all men have not only an innate dread of superior talents, which is to be calmed only by obsequiousness, but also so much of the *amor sui* that they soon fall into a partiality towards those who are inferior, provided their applications be decked in a winning garb. of manner and address.

And, oh! if you have discernment! There are some clergymen CALLED *Saints*—they love flattery, and the plainest clothes imaginable. Some are called *orthodox*—they must be won by a straight-forward and manly pretension, coupled with a sufficient *posse* of testimonials. Some are called *high-churchmen*—they are by far most difficult—they require a tremendous load of proof touching your piety, learning, experience, ability, active habits, rigid morality: but, then they are equally more liberal, and generally spurn any notion of offering less than an ample stipend. With all, however, whether you write or speak, that sort of urbane, respectful bearing, which appears in the style of St. Paul, will go farther than any other quality I know.

But, all this preface belongs to the fact that, being invited to dine with a brother-curate one day, to meet a few friends, I casually heard of a curacy vacant, with the advantage, so long desired, of a residence;

and my application was, after probation, crowned with success.

This exaltation, which at once doubled my income, carried us from a large, populous place of manufacture, to one of those little market-towns, in which scandal loves to dwell, and where every person is proverbially engaged in every other person's business; and, after having established ourselves once more, we found these properties attached to it in a very decided manner. But, though at first it was somewhat annoying to hear of all the fabrications, slanders and misrepresentations which flourished in this little hot-bed, a short time enabled us to treat them with merited indifference. Much kindness, from the few, who were raised above the rest, supported us against the malice of the many who were chiefly professed dissenters of one kind or other; although it is worthy of note, that one of the most friendly families was that of the poor but very worthy minister of one of these sects; and up to this period, now nearly three years, the best possible understanding exists be tween us.*

* I lament that this worthy man has been recently discharged by his flock, on account of his poverty—as I have been credibly informed: but, as he himself informed me, because he was too friendly towards the established Church—"their great enemy."

I shall offer a short description of this, the new seat of my labours.

Being in a district eminently agricultural, the parishioners are, in the bulk, rustics—farmers, cottagers, and labourers; but there are attorneys, surgeons, and some few widow and maiden ladies who live on their means—the last-mentioned contributing much both to the welfare of the establishment, and to the propagation of what is called *gossip*, being *ladies-patronesses* of the national school, assisting and sometimes interfering in the Curate's affairs of visiting the sick and needy, doing, upon the whole, a great deal of good with not very much harm, and living in a state of the most blissful self-satisfaction. One-half of the parish may be considered the poor, who are (for the more part, though by no means alone) extremely profligate, despisers of dignities, and, as I believe to my sorrow, generally without any religion at all—this last, to my entire conviction, being the consequence of dissent and want of municipal authority.

With regard to the former cause, however invidious any remarks from me would appear, I cannot forbear presenting to my reader an extract which I make from the " *Protestant Reformation* " of that very clever and ingenious writer — the late Mr. Cobbett; because it contains more of the bitterness of truth than I am willing, in my own language, to display.

" I ask the UNITARIAN parson, or prater, for instance, why he takes upon him that office; why he does not go and follow some trade, or why he does not work in the fields. His answer is, that he is more usefully employed in teaching. If I ask, of *what* use his teaching is, he tells me, he must tell me, that his teaching is *necessary to the salvation of souls.* Well, say I, but, why not leave that business to the established church, to which the people all pay tithes? Oh, no! says he, I cannot do that, because the church does not teach the *true religion.* Well, say I; but, true or false, if it *serve for salvation,* what signifies it? Here I have him penned up in a corner. He is compelled to confess, that he is a fellow wanting to lead an easy life, by pandering to the passions or whims of conceited persons; or, to insist, that his sort of belief and teaching are *absolutely necessary to salvation:* as he will not confess the former, he is obliged to insist on the latter: and here, after all his railing against the *intolerance* of the Catholics, he maintains the doctrine of *exclusive salvation.*"—(Lett. vii.)

A conscientious dissenter, who bridleth his tongue, is a man whom I heartily respect. To such, neither the words of the departed M.P. nor I have any just ground of objection. But the melancholy cause of schism in the body of professing Christians is to be found in that mutual and tacit covenant of support which exists between the preachers and the hearers. Those are willing to live by their ministry; these are ready, from the common love of change and novelty, to vindicate their *right of choice* by leaving the good old paths for new ones of their own. The great mass of dissenters, in such districts as this, cannot be guided by any scruples of conscience; for their ignorance is too great, and their carelessness of life too striking to permit it to be supposed that they ever exercise any mental judgment in religious matters. For instance, one man will not suffer his apprentice to be *confirmed* by the Bishop, *because he does not believe in it;* another goes to the *meeting*, because he has had a misunderstanding with the parish clerk; and a third, because he is conscious of having been a grievous sinner, goes to hear preached the (to him) comfortable doctrine of absolute and unconditional election—while the convenience of sitting in pews, like the gentlefolks at church, has a great excellence in the eyes of many.

But, letting these things pass, the other cause of want of religion was said to be the want of municipal authority. Where there is no one to uphold the laws with regard to those minor offences which private individuals seldom trouble themselves to take before the magistrate, the value of character soon falls, and public nuisances are practised with impunity.

The remedy for either of these causes is not at hand. They exist in and by the general spirit of discontent and insubordination which is now (with the school-master) abroad—a spirit which pervades every class, living upon the licentiousness of the press, and the general diffusion of *useful* (to use the term) *knowledge,* and now glorying in such a palmy state that, as all attempts to extinguish it would only give it strength and fierceness, so the necessity which remains is to drive forward those causes which have produced it, under the old adage that all extremes meet at the same point. A monster has been brought into ex-istence, and its makers tremble while they feed it with all manner of dainty food, in the hope (if hope they have) of destroying it by repletion.

Let us, however, confine ourselves to the little scene of which I undertook to attempt a description—the picture is in no measure finished, because I have yet to put in a figure which will give a complexion to the whole.

There is, in this little town, a school; and, as this establishment is conducted by a D.D., and other dis-tinguished scholars, the reader will readily suppose it a proud addition to our community. An addition it certainly is; but it is an *incubus,* by the breath of which every part of the body, except such as either delight in corruption, or are insensible to all infection, is morally disgusted. During eight months of the year, the streets are continually infested with the young gentlemen, who seem to enjoy unbounded licence out of school-hours, and point the finger, or shoot the lip, as every passer-by is considered worthy of their notice. They are sent to church, forsooth, because most of them are *intended for the ministry;* but, while there, being free, often from any *nominal,* and always from all *actual surveillance,* they amuse themselves — the more sedate — with reading such books as they like to bring with them—the more vivacious—with such conduct as would be tolerated only between the acts in a play-house; taking occasion always at the time of singing, either to destroy all devotion by their obstreperous clamour, under the cloak of joining in the psalm, or to keep up a lively conversation and course of remarks upon the congregation below.

The head-master of this school is, as was said, a D.D. and, as far as I can judge, a friend of Dissenters, a lover of radicalism, and not very warmly attached to that *church-and-state* establishment by and through which he has acquired great riches, his present office, all his celebrity, his scarlet gown, and a college living. The other masters appear to be any thing but permanent officers, though they have good salaries and very little to do. How much of the

moral delinquency of the parish is not clearly de-
ducible from this impure fountain? If example have
any weight with the ignorant, and if young men,
between sixteen and twenty years of age, require any
restraints, the reader may judge for himself. But,
let me so far qualify what is said with reference to
this school, which is a sore burthen upon me, as to
make honourable exception in favour of the few
young men in it who seem steadily to bear up against
the current of contagion, and have hitherto escaped
the general *rot*. They are few, but they are fine
fellows, and will one day be ornaments of usefulness
to society: and, while I can look upon something—
some *spem gregis*, I shall not despair, even though, as
a little sharp-shins, going to Eton, once said of the
guard of the coach as he gave himself up to a bundle
of straw for the night, *malus pastor dormit supinus*.

CHAPTER XIX.

Though Fortune's malice overthrow my state,
My mind exceeds the compass of her wheel.
SHAKSPEARE.

IF the reader has perused the last chapter, he will be inclined to set the writer down for one as discontented as may be, and in as-ill a humour as possible. No: I am very thankful that, notwithstanding all that is against me, I can truly say, "The lot is fallen unto me in a fair ground: yea, I have a goodly heritage." For, besides much evil, there is sufficient good to make me content; and, though deprived of much usefulness by the disaffection of the many, I can retire into the bosom of my family, where I am all to them, and there enjoy the assurance of a quiet conscience. Practised in the school of experience, the writer returns from the death-bed, around which stood pert sectarians, without any feeling of bitterness; and, while he reads the purely scriptural service for the burial of the dead, before those whom necessity alone has brought to hear, he can lift his soul to heaven, despite the masked hypocrite at his side, unfettered by the coarse links of worldly feeling. The cynical sneer of the hostile, the empty gaze of the indifferent, or the smothered jests of the destitute —amidst so many sects—of all religious impressions —all dissenters from the *Church religion* (as the poor souls express themselves), because they can escape unseen in the motley crowd, and attach themselves to any or no denomination—these once had an effect which they have not now. The surface of the lake, in summer, exhibits the effect of every fitful breeze, and every little gust can throw it into motion; but, when less halcyon days succeed, a ruffled consistency is proof against these desultory interruptions; and yet the surface is as pleasing to the eye, and as serviceable to the objects of creation, as it is undisturbed and even in its general aspect. So, let it not be imputed that I have become lukewarm in a service which demands unflinching energy; or that I have settled down in a merely specious discharge of duties which involve the whole power of the unseen workings of the mind.

I have yielded to that which no power of mine can stand against—" the time is out of joint;" and, leaving it in the hands of One that is mighty, *do find* contentment in the conscientious discharge of duty as far as this duty is permitted to be done. *The spirit of the age* has been declared to be the ruler of the nation; and, if we must needs submit to such an ugly tyranny, opposition would certainly be fruitless—better to pay some outward deference to his ethereal majesty, and live in hopes—for, " perchance, 'twill walk again"—of a mortification from excessive cold.

A steady adherence to duty, with an unwavering determination never to compromise those feelings which arise from a careful discrimination between *right* and *wrong*, must, unless the wisdom of our Creator designs to visit His people with the rod of adversity, triumph over the wretched coalition between every thing *doubtful* and every thing *bad*. I declare that I am of no *party;* but, assuming to myself the common right of judging in matters which pertain to conscience and opinion, it is my purpose never to consent to the substitution of evil for good, or bitter for sweet.

Returning to the tiny stream of my biography, it is time that something was said of my new *employer*—for this term even is more palatable than the abused ones which are commonly adopted. *You are my Curate; I am your Rector*—amounts to this;—a person is said to be *under the care of one whom he rules.*

My new employer is a man wholly bent upon doing, and having done, that which is right; but, because he is of noble family, and derives the income of his benefice from the land which the people rent and occupy *on this condition,* he is unpopular. His mode of life differing from mine as much as the Equator from the Pole, we are most harmoniously united in the work of the ministry, and (to use the diction of our parishioners) as long as I must have *a master,* I never wish for a better. Liberal, just, courteous, and affable, he is all (as far as my own wishes go) he need be; and I covet neither the lineage of his ancestry, nor the splendour of his associates. We are distinct, yet blended—unassociated, yet yoked together.

But if, notwithstanding the paradox which is just above, there is any disunion between *us,* how great is the want of compact among the clergy generally. I am now going to take leave of all distinctions, such as those which exist between *beneficed* and *non-beneficed* ministers—this distinction being only with regard to fortune, and, therefore, not to be admitted in any essay soberly undertaken—and, as I promised, to offer some observations upon this evil in our establishment.

In the world, *rich* men lord it over *poor;* and he who rides in his coach is many inches higher than he whom he meets a pedestrian on the road; but, though the same—actually the same—contrast may be drawn between the wealthiest and the poorest of the parochial clergy, it ought to fall, to vanish like smoke, before the radiant spirit of Christianity. A community of goods, I am not (shall I say) fanatic enough to aim at; but I will aim directly at a community of *feeling*, which should cause to operate an interchange of brotherly visits, a reciprocity of encouraging, cheering intercourse. Is there any thing like it? My own case shall answer for me; and (mark you, gentle reader,) I am an exemplary, well-approved, and talented clergyman, or the world has much abused my credulity. Every man knows pretty much of himself; and, therefore, I ask no indulgence for this apparent conceit.

I have been some years in my present residence, and yet I am not upon *friendly* terms with *any one* of my clerical brethren. I don't know *three*, even upon speaking terms; and yet there are *fifty* within ten miles. There are " saints," enthusiasts, zealots; but, some of them are *Hon.s*, and some are *Dons;* some have married wives with money and are very genteel; some are allied to titles and hold family livings ; but I am poor, married to a poor woman, and come of a poor (albeit, a highly respectable and ancient) family. There are fox-hunters and fortune-hunters; but as I always despised the pursuit of the one, so have I no relish for the chase of the other; and am, moreover, *only a curate.* There are old men and young men, high-born and low-born; but I have nothing to do with them. We might be, respectively, the ministers of all the religions under the sun, and, as far as I am concerned, no farther removed from active brotherly love.

Now the evil of all this, to any one individually, it would perhaps be difficult to find; but, who sees not the evil to the church—if it be right to call that evil which is not good? What a glorious banner would it be upon the battlements of our strong-hold, if we could really inscribe the word *brotherly-love* in the eyes of the dissenters! What dismay would seize on their distracted bands, if the clergy of a district were bound hand-in-hand, and, by their intercourse, encouraged one another in the performance of their arduous duties!

But, there is much *positive evil.* The rich clergy do not hang to the poor, and the lynx-eyed people see it: the poor clergy are despised, and the people borrow the idea. Why despised? Because they are unnoticed. Why not hang to them? Because they never come near them in their humbler abodes—

because they *do not know* them. Why! the clergy of a diocese ought to be the children of one family; and the bishop—alas! this calls to mind another sore—as their " father" indeed.

It is surely a bad and queer excuse, to say that, perhaps, the calls of the one might not be acceptable to the other class. If there be a clergyman ashamed, before a brother, of his noble poverty; or, on the other hand, one elated with worldly greatness, he can have but little of the spirit which ought to inspire his thoughts and actions. Let them come and see us, not for our sake, but for the sake of those entrusted to our care; and we promise them that, if they will excuse our littleness, their neighing steeds and polished carriage shall stand at our door without being coveted, or they may walk away, as great in their own, and much greater in our estimation than before.

But, the bishop?—Well, I must say all; because the good of my country is the prize which even this little book aspires to.

Hampered in circumstances, and dreading the extremities of legal persecution, I wrote a series of sermons, with a view of publishing by subscription. What more natural than that I should desire the countenance of the bishop over me? What more excusable than that I should also presume to ask for it? But, however, before I proceeded upon these impulses, it appeared advisable to seek the recommendation of that bishop of whom mention was made in the early part of this work ; and the rather, because I yet considered that I had a claim upon his kindness. With wonted courtesy, he complied, provided that my own diocesan sanctioned the proceeding ; but my own diocesan pithily replied, that he had never given his sanction to works on divinity since his elevation to the episcopal dignity, and declined. I then renewed my petition, upon the score of the other bishop's provisional compliance, with all the tact and deference which I could invent ; but my letter—my petition—my prayer—remains unnoticed to this day.

Thus left with but one string to my bow, I returned to my former diocesan—him at whose hands I received both orders. I wrote to him, explaining all the circumstances, and begging, nevertheless, to be allowed the privilege of placing his name at the head of my list. But the string went and the bow was broken. I was in London, partly for the purpose of setting my work off, when my wife sent me this bishop's answer in the negative, written by his secretary (either his son or his daughter), with all the manœuvring and generalship of *Scrub* in the *Stratagem*.

Now, all this is not as it ought to be. The *bishops* must be *paternal* in their regard for the inferior *clergy*

—the inferior clergy must be *fraternal* in their regard for each other; or the church, IF it fall—fall when it may—will be found to have had this mortal wound in its vitals—the want of unity—the *house*, if not *divided against itself*, not well cemented together. Depend upon it, the real enemies to the church are to be found among its pledged supporters.

CHAPTER XX.

Sorrowing most of all for the words which he spake,
that they should see his face no more.

ACTS.

B——'s accounts of his parish, poor fellow! were hitherto summer accounts, and all was cheering and delightful. They had witnessed an occasional swell in the ocean, and his public ministrations had been sometimes accompanied with the roar of their august and mighty neighbour. The long dark nights of autumn had brought out the coast-guard service, and some few of *Dirk Hatterick's* tribe had already paid a visit to " the parson's house;" for B—— one morning found under the drawing-room window a small cask of precious *Cognac* directed to " His Reverence," which was placed there, no doubt, with something like the feeling which prompted a sop for Cerberus—

as the inoffensive character of the clergyman had led
him, in all former days, never to divulge the secret
that some odd times, the garden had been made the
retreat by night of the smugglers, and some high and
very thick bushes of laurel and " the hardy laurus-
tinus" formed a sort of cove for sundry kegs and
bales which it might not, at all times, have been quite
convenient to carry further into the interior, for a day
or two.

But *winter* came, and B———'s constitution could
not stand the winds. He had long laboured against
cold after cold, and continual coughs; but one day
at the burial of a corpse, he received, it was supposed,
the ground-work of a serious illness. His physician
declared that his life would be, at least annually, jeo-
parded, if he remained in his present situation, and
advised, by all means, that he should procure a
curate, and become a non-resident for, at all events,
half of every year.

B———, however, was not the man to commit the
sacred trust of his flock to a *hireling;* and his own
finances would not allow him to make for a deputy-
curate that provision to which his services would en-
title him.   (N. B. *hireling* means a gentleman of
education, who receives from fifty to eighty
pounds a-year for the occupation of his time and
talents; *deputy-curate* denotes one who is paid so

liberally that he is able to make the appearance, and keep up the character of the curate whose place he supplies, whose services he performs, and whose importance he ought to sustain). When he got well, he determined upon an exchange of preferment, the health of Julia as well as of himself rendering this step absolutely necessary. This was soon effected—the situation was full of attractions to many; and B——'s farewell sermon was delivered, with tears on his pale and care-worn cheeks, to a congregation of the whole parish, among whom not one underwent the trial without at least a glistening eye.

"Think not, my friends," said he, "that the moments, as they pass, rush into that oblivion of darkness which is the commonly awarded fate of all the time that is gone; or that, as they go away, so do the deeds, by which they are signalized, sink into the death of forgetfulness. Ah! no. They will return each bringing back the testimony of its former being—the sins which we commit, or the negligences of which we are guilty now, will then appear, when the books shall be opened, and *Time*, declared finished by the angel's hand lift up to heaven, *shall be no longer.*"

At one time, alluding to the mortality which had, both by sea and land, marked that winter in the recollection of his parishioners, he thus insinuated the duty of submitting to the decrees of Heaven. "Then,

children of sorrow !—ye, whose parents have led you
the way to the portals of eternal life—widows ! whose
partners tarry for you in a happier and no very distant
clime—parents ! bereaved of the tender plants from
which ye thought to gather much good fruit—check, oh
check, and subdue this rising storm ! *The Lord gave—*
and it may be you have long enjoyed the boon—*The
Lord hath taken away*—and can it be, that you would
stand face to face with the will of God, and murmur
at his determination ? If the path, which you would
have chosen, be obstructed, remember that it is ' the
angel of the Lord standing in the way, and his sword
drawn in his hand.' You cannot pass. It is God's
will ; and is it not then a pleasing, a soothing, a heal-
ing balm to your hurt minds, to say and *feel*, ' Thy
will, O Lord, be done !' "

He, at another time, chid their too great hankering
after the things of life, by an allusion to our Saviour's
inquiry, when in a storm on the sea of Tiberias,
" Where is your faith ?" " We see," said the young
preacher, " it is true, many cheering examples of a virtuous life, in which the more interesting duties of our
social state are performed with zeal and fidelity, and
incorporated with the grand work of Christianity ;
and, so far, it is well. But, when we come to the
test,—when, what we have passed off with so much
benefit to others, as current gold, is cast into the fur-

nace of *affliction*—then, *where is our Faith?* Now, I pray you, mark the difference. If, with meekness and resignation, we bend our necks before the Almighty Giver of all things—if, while the unavailing tear bespeaks the sensibility of the generous heart, we turn our streaming eyes to heaven, and say, ' O Lord, thy will be done!'—our *faith* is—what? It is like *the Son of God*—it rises above the turmoil of the storm, and *calms* the sorrows which it has no tendency or intention to *destroy*. On the contrary, if the storm continue, the Saviour sleeps—that is, the grace of our Lord Jesus Christ is dormant in our hearts; but, if this grace be awakened—if we really call to mind that God, not man, is the Ruler of the world, then shall the Saviour's ' still small voice' be heard in the conflict of the breast—' Rest, rest; perturbed spirit! It is thy God that hath done this great thing! It is thy God that bids thee, *Peace, be still!*'"

Here some weather-beaten sailors rose from their seats, wiped their eyes, and gazed inquiringly in the face of poor B——, whose nerves were sadly, though honourably, shaken; and, as if taking a hint from them, though his sermon was not extempore, but, according to the good taste which is due to the present character of the English church, written before him, he proceeded :—

" If the bewildered crew of some devoted transport, when winds and waves seemed leagued in direful compact to destroy them, were suddenly to find themselves surrounded by friendly life-boats, and to have sure reason to expect deliverance from the raging storm; we should, indeed, be astonished to see them still bewailing their unhappy fate, and, rather than avail themselves of proffered safety, clinging to the sinking wreck. How much more, in the storms of life, when all the feelings of the natural man are tossed together in fearful conflict, should we wonder, when we see the professed followers of Christ still clinging to the clay of death, while life—' the life'— the immortal and eternal life—cries, ' Come unto me —O ye of little faith, wherefore do ye doubt?' Why, my friends, we have heard some of you, while with gallant hearts and helping hands the fainting wreck has been cleared by you of its frail tenants— we have heard your loud acclamations of joy, amid the crash and roar of elements, and ye have cried, ' thank God!' when every soul was landed on an earthly shore. Think, then, of how much more importance is that eternal salvation, the Lord of which comes forth to meet you, and to save you, in the storms and conflicts of the world—to preserve you, not from earthly ruin, but from the jaws of an eternal hell beneath!''

Such passages were delivered, as they were felt,

with energy; and I, who was among the assembled throng, whose sobs now filled the little sea-coast tabernacle with holy sorrow, and seemed the earnest of a victory over sin and everlasting ruin, could no longer sit upon my seat, when, with a calm and dignified demeanour, yet meek and prepossessing as a lamb, B———, collecting all his mastership, reiterated thus the burthen of his text :—

" And now, behold, I know that ye all, among whom I have gone preaching the kingdom of God, shall see my face no more. Wherefore I take you to record this day, that I am pure from the blood of all men. For 1 have not shunned to declare unto you all the counsel of God," Acts xx. 25.

I now cast my eyes round the church. From the tenants of my Lady ———'s pew, to the group of poor old men and women who had, by this time, collected round the foot of the stairs to the pulpit, not a dry eye was to be seen; while many, and many ladies in particular, honestly buried their faces in their hands and handkerchiefs and wept audibly. I thought our Sion had not fallen *yet*, and could not stifle a suppressed ejaculation—*Behold, how they love one another!* But, how shall I render its own force to that passage in which he reminded his beloved flock :—

" The disciples of Jesus were asked, amid the thunders of the storm of Tiberias, where *their* hopes were placed, and in what *their* confidence was centred: but conscience will ask you, and me, when the clouds of death already darken the horizon of our life, and when the roar of eternity's boundless ocean breaks upon our dying ears, *Where is your faith?* And what answer will you give?—for it is an inquiring counsellor, and it must be answered. What balm can allay the pangs of an importunate spirit like this—what is the harbour, in sight of which the soul may safely launch into the depths, and shoot the fearful falls, of an eternal existence? Truly, it is the belief in Jesus—it is the trust under the shadow of his wings—it is the hearing of that voice which says—'Come unto me, all ye that labour, and are heavy laden, and I will give you rest.'"

I felt relieved when the discourse was thus finished. I felt for B——, I felt for his audience. But, oh! they were feelings which one would not exchange for a diadem of earthly greatness. Never did I feel so proudly sensible of the Saviour's counsel—"Ye are the salt of the earth." Never did I feel so ready to endure the cross, and count all things but dung for the excellency thereof. There was a stillness, deeper than the gloom into which the protracted length of the sermon had brought us, when, as the lips of a frail man uttered it, there seemed to fall on every downcast head, "*The Peace of God,* which passeth all understanding;" and, as poor B—— raised his streaming eyes, the evening star, now risen bright, seemed to lend them a temporary beam, as he went through the rest of that form; until, when his voice had faultered over " Be amongst you," and he had buried them in his two hands, the remainder was all but a whisper, yet so audible, while he sank upon his knees and breathed *" and remain with you always!"*

That evening was one, never to be forgotten by the inhabitants of P——; and, in attestation of the general feeling, many were the suitors who, in addition to the party at the rectory-house, came to beg one more adieu from their beloved pastor.

———

B——'s preferment was exchanged; but nothing, at all eligible, had been offered for it, but an incumbency in Ireland. It was in the south of the island, but in a district which had not been subject to any great disturbance or rebellion; whereas, the offers of preferment in our own island were from the colliery or pottery districts, and B——'s health could never bear the discharge of the duties devolved upon a clergyman, where the population is not only vast, but entirely ignorant, and given to sensuality: or they were from large parishes in large towns; as Nottingham, where sixty thousand souls and more are confided to one man together with his assistants;

and the same objection existed: or they were from remote districts in the west or north of England, remarkable either for some glaring eye-sore, such as an unhealthy, marshy situation, or from some peculiar difficulty in the raising of the income.

All things duly considered, the Irish rectory was fixed upon; and, with a good heart, both B—— and his wife embarked for a settlement in a land against which so much had been, as they conceived, very unjustly said.

It was soon found that the importance of B——'s affairs, in his new residence, was such as to require the aid of a gentleman who could manage the department of land and tithe agent; and as the brother of our wives was glad to have an opportunity of being near one whom he loved as well, if not as dearly as his sisters, little persuasion was necessary to induce him to accept the office.

Every thing upon their arrival had borne a favourable aspect. The peasantry came in flocks to welcome their coming; and the bells of the church, situate in a warm and healthy vale, rang a long and merry peal upon the occasion. The Roman catholic priest of the parish (for it was about equally divided between papists and protestants), came, and, with honest sincerity and friendliness, proffered any assistance in his power until B—— should become

acquainted with the localities of the parish and neighbourhood. My friend was not the man to lose a
friend on the score of any difference in matters of conscience, and they entered at once upon a good understanding which was never infringed. Though an
Irishman, educated at Maynooth, he, nevertheless,
had something like culture about him; and, above
all, had a great share of the good taste which leads
one *not to display* those religious peculiarities which
are not acceptable to another.

And every thing went on well. The letters we
received were comforting and satisfactory—they were
hardly less interesting.

"These people," said B——, "of course I
mean the great mass—the peasantry—such as we
have seen in England, thronging our public ways
about the time of harvest—are not bad—nay, they
have a generosity of heart and sentiment and action,
which, were it not subject to sudden storms of elevation, in which it becomes vengeance in behalf of their
friends, would be worthy of unqualified admiration.
Various causes may be alleged for their mental, as
well as actual, inferiority in the scale of society; not
one of which can, alone, account, even in any degree,
for the result, as far as my observation and opinion
go. They are behind, far behind us, *mentally*, because, in the main, their religious creed imposes igno-

rance, and their priests take care to exact submission;—because, by habit, they renounce, or rather
never embrace, the idea of thinking for themselves,
and, if they could, would cease to be accountable
agents;—because they are degraded by their own
consent, giving up to others the very keeping of
their consciences, and believing, or assenting to, the
doctrine of infallibility in the rulers of the church to
which they belong. And they are behind us in all
other respects; partly from the causes already mentioned; partly from others, which are numerous
indeed.

" Among the most prominent of these causes may
be considered (I think) their addiction to ardent
spirits; absenteeism, by which too great a prepon-
derance, in numbers, is given to the lowest class; the
baneful system of underletting, by which the burthen
of tithes is thrown upon the same class, not by the
clergy of our establishment, but by their own Roman
catholic brethren in prosperity; party-spirit, which
promotes idleness and dissipation; and the present
system of *agitation*, by which a few, living chiefly out
of the country, are the only persons benefited in a
pecuniary point of view, and a great many, living
wholly out of the country, are deterred from returning to it, and prefer the commission of their houses
and estates to grinding underlings, while the bulk of

their incomes goes to feed the hungry foreigner, or to swell the wealth of old England.

" In a consideration of their religious condition nothing strikes us more forcibly than the deep-rooted —nay, the inexpugnable conviction which they entertain that they, as well as we, are indebted to popery for Christianity—that, before what they call the mission from Pope Gregory in the end of the sixth century, the Gospel had never reached the British Isles. Amazing effrontery! and yet this is a prejudice so firmly fixed in the minds of the better sort (for the lowest know or care nothing about it), and, I should think, of the bulk of their priests, that all efforts to eradicate it would appear hopeless."

CHAPTER XXI.

Severity breaks the mind ; and then, in the place of a disorderly young fellow, you have a low-spirited moped creature.

LOCKE.

How comes this poverty, with double income, Mr Curate ? will be the natural inquiry. Indeed, I have, in order to bring into the last chapter but one all I had to say against the clergy, gone so far a-head of my due position, that it is necessary to return to the period at which I pitched my tent in the little town of which so much has been said.

Though small, for a town, it was so much more considerable than the villages in which I had hitherto officiated, that the services of the church were at once deeply interesting, and sufficient to keep me in daily employment. The interment of the dead—that office which brings the minister into a connection with his parishioners so affecting and affectionate—was now, upon an average, every week; the visiting of the sick, both voluntarily and by request, made me more acquainted with the stirring influence of approaching or expected death: nor were my visits to the poor, albeit oftentimes rendered less satisfactory by their mouthy protestations in favour of the " Church-religion," without a measure of satisfaction which well repaid me. In fact, I was studious to win the best feelings of the people; punctual in attending to all their calls; dividing my time between my parish and my family (the latter having now become more considerable from the acquisition of a son); never dreaming of ill-will, either *pro* or *con;* doing my duty, far beyond the letter; and deriving to myself that sweetener of life—a good and approving conscience.

Things had gone on in this way for some four months, when a blow came which entirely changed the aspect of my affairs—a blow which cannot fail, under any circumstances, of awakening the sleeping faculties of both mind and body; but which, in my posture, brought at once the moral image of all those feelings which may be supposed to rush into the mind of him who, from being in the rear, suddenly comes into the van of a contending army, and sees the various forms of destruction with his living eyes— hitherto he had heard the roar of cannon and, as he advanced, trampled over the wounded and the dead; now he beholds the deadly weapons of his enemies, marks their terrible machines, and discerns their grim and eager features—it was the death of my father. For some weeks, he had complained of bodily pain and oppression; but, so little, until the last week, in which he had an instinctive assurance of his fate, that every arrangement was made for his visit to us on the christening of our first child. According to our popular superstition, the new suit was made, and carefully reserved for the festal day; alas! the summons came, and his raiment was the shroud.

This visitation exchanged my state of confiding assurance to one of dependence upon the mercy and forbearance of the world. Various responsibilities, in which my father and I had been joined, fell wholly upon me; a load of debt descended; and, in a word, there rushed upon me, through the flood-gates of this event, that tide of dunning and suing, with which I am even now struggling, unsubdued indeed, but yet exposed to the danger of being dragged under by any one of the remaining monsters which seem to take their cold-blooded pastime in its eddying waters. This, then, brought poverty and, which is infinitely worse, perplexity.

I now besought the incumbent, with whom I was engaged, to cancel, from the articles of our agreement, that which prohibited me from taking pupils. He acceded to a degree just higher than nothing, by which it was next to impossible that I could be benefited; for every person must know that *one* pupil, unless upon terms which not one parent in ten thousand can accede to, would not profit one. I blame not him, but the wretched policy upon which his decision rests. Can any man do his duty—nay, half his duty, when it consists mainly in mental energy—if his mind be in a constant state of perturbation and uncertainty, not knowing that the next month may not consign him to a gaol? And, again, every one, who has ever been engaged in a daily employment, such as teaching, must admit that a person so engaged is much more likely to perform the duties of a collateral and congenial, though a paramount office with credit, than one who has merely those duties imposed upon a life of comparative leisure.

Whatever a man takes to, as the means of filling up his time, if it be not a duty, will speedily become all engrossing, be it *reading, writing,* or *gardening—fishing, fiddling,* or *fox-hunting;* but, being a *duty,* it is thrown aside when over, and leaves the habit and disposition in a healthy state of activity. Some few men there may be in the world who can sit waiting like a yawning porter in his lodge for the arrival of any duty, and while away the intervals in the laborious employment of doing nothing; but, not of this sort, I must be after something.

The recitals of lying and slandering which came by this time to our ears; and hypocrisy, which now too often met my eyes, had their due effect in adding to the deteriorating influence which poverty and disappointment had upon my mental, and, through them, upon my professional exertions. I had not seen, in all their force, the many proofs in Scripture that such have ever been the loop-holes through which human depravity loves to etrude its reckless—yet winning aspect.

David describeth a citizen of Zion in the following words :—"Lord, who shall abide in thy tabernacle? who shall dwell in thy holy hill? He that walketh uprightly, and worketh righteousness, and *speaketh the truth in his heart : he that backbiteth not with his tongue,* nor doeth evil to his neighbour; *nor taketh up a reproach against his neighbour,*" (Psalm xv.); and I know of no words which convey so forcibly the indignation of the God of Truth against the common practice of our own luminous age. He, who bare our infirmities, left on record his denunciation, in that he apostrophized our great enemy as " *the Father of lies;*" and, as if to impress the mind with a deep sense of the enormity of a crime which is, in general, beyond the reach of earthly redress, the very last chapter of the sacred records—nay, the very last words, as far as the rule of our lives is laid down, are these:—" Blessed are they that do His commandments, that they may have right to the tree of life, and may enter in through the gates into the city. For without are dogs, and sorcerers, and whoremongers, and murderers, and idolaters, and *whosoever loveth and maketh a lie.*"

A due attention to this fact will wean many a persecuted mind from that natural clinging to the *on dits* of a world sunk in depravity, and will enable it, not only to bear up against, but to triumph over and defeat, the malignity of that monster—*common report.* " What all the world says," far from being so well entitled to belief that it "must be true," will soon appear to him quite as likely, at least, to be utterly false. But I had not *then* so learned the world, by the help of those Scriptures which were, indeed, " written for our learning."

The *funeral,* even, appeared not always now that occasion of Christian sympathy and heavenward piety which it seemed at first—I say *seemed;* for my inexperience of people wholly depraved, had hitherto kept me in ignorance of reality. Exceptions, indeed, must be made from this as a general swoop; and they were most visible, when some poor, bending widow followed the parish-coffin; or a mother, bereft of the tender pledge of conjugal felicity, had no connexion in her grief with the remaining world. Too often, a whole troop of Dissenters and their wives, each with a handkerchief to hide the hardness of a flinty countenance, and each hired to the pomp by a gratuity of silk and gloves, would follow one to the grave, at the side of which I stood the mere tool of their necessity, not only unpropitiated by this trumpery, but even grudged the right by which I acted. Another time, some stingy churchman, in order to pay him the compliment of scarf and hat-band, and escape the expense of a two-fold gift, would request the incumbent to perform the ceremony, saying that the deceased had expressed a wish to that effect, which, I observe, is never said of any of the poor. Then the offspring of imprudence or depravity was brought, with real rejoicing but "the mockery of woe," to engage the service of the church. Such instances almost absorbed the sense of feeling which must exert itself when real piety and holy resignation bring its exacted victims to the tomb; and, I began to slide into that official formality inseparable from all human institutions.

As to visiting the poor, it was now growing manifest that the silver *coda*, which closed my *pastorale*, was to them by far the most, if not the only, desirable part of the business; and that, when this was a-wanting, I might have had back again all my pains. Here, again, I am cautioned to announce the exceptions, but the general rule is too clearly defined to allow even *charity* to draw a veil over it. To the *sick*, of course, I went whenever I was called in, and continued my visits with regularity until death or recovery: often I went voluntarily, and, so long as I was received cordially, repeated the office. Nothing, I trust, will ever operate so as to render this duty less than deeply and entirely interesting and engaging; but, as to many of the poor and needy (so called), I must confess, often have I been tempted to leave them in that hopeless state of levelling and dissenting ignorance in which I found them. I regret this, but it is so: and one chief cause is, that necessity compels me to be much at home and in my garden, (a man who has a family and not the means of keeping a supply of servants, must do many things for himself, and his little ones), to study hard for the bread which perisheth, and to devise and execute various means of gaining deliverance from my remaining embarrassments.

One thing, however, has never shewn a tendency to desert me. I continue to discharge, with utmost zeal and pains, the public offices of divine service, and am happy enough, in these days even, to find my ministrations well attended.

The Dissenters send for me to *name* their children, under the pretence of sickness, but evidently only with an eye to the benefit of being registered, or, in the event of death, of burial in the church-yard; and I go never failing to make an exhortation on the necessity of bringing them afterwards to church, which is (I fear) as regularly treated with contempt.

But, even under all these circumstances of trial, and though my difficulties have gone on, with various modifications of writs, threats, insults, on the part of those claimants who yet remained unpaid, down to the present moment, I thank my God that I am even better off than many who deserve much more; and, with regard to my office, the things connected with it pass on in a train much more even and undisturbed, as well as much more satisfactory, than falls to the lot of the majority of my brethren in the ministry. I have rather attempted to show cause why I am not in a perfection of human blessedness, than to complain of what is really the case.

But, to revert to the event which opened the way to a host of calamities, it also brought about me my family. There was some, and there might have been vast, comfort in this; but more of what would gladly have been dispensed with. Had I married a rich woman, (this was the amount,) I might have afforded a harbour for some, while others might have been enabled to pursue an idle or unprofitable life. I was suddenly discovered to be the prop, always designed by my late father to support, in case of need, our tottering house; while, at the same time, my college expenses, for half of which debts were unpaid and have come duly upon my own head, were laid against me with much more than due precision. The reader will not accuse me of casting any unfilial reflections upon the memory of a dear and affectionate parent.

It must not, however, be said—"here is a man, in *debt*—the consequence of his own extravagance—and *poverty*—the companion of debt—who quarrels with his profession and its duties—his superiors, his equals, and his inferiors." It is not so.—Were there, generally, a befitting remuneration for the curate's, or assistant-curate's, services, or were he allowed an universal right (which appears an inalienable right) to increase his pittance by all becoming means, my really small load of debt could have been disbanded in a year or two, and my poverty turned to riches by frugality. But the grand source of misery is this— to be called upon by impatient creditors, each concluding that *now* is the nick of time to get his money, to do that which is impossible—with one hundred pounds due at the end of a year, to pay down one hundred and fifty pounds at the beginning, and support one's family into the bargain; and to be cut off, at the same time, from all means of increasing his income. If people saw you in a state *to pay*, they would take your engagements; but, supposing you not in this state, and seeing *no irons in the fire*, from the ill grounded fear of your employer that you will burn your fingers, they press what appears their only hope with desperate firmness. You strive and borrow, implore, assure; a small income is consumed in postages; you, at your wits' end, dread the sweeping consummation which a certain *act* offers, as an everlasting *stigma;* and, with such a spurring and goading at your sides, such a slashing across your shoulders, and such thumps about the head, you are expected to go through your work with mill-horse patience and regularity.

He must, indeed, be made of most unfeeling stuff who does not sink, some few degrees, beneath such a yoke, and who does not find some fault with the regulations of a church which leave the *working clergy* to the caprice of some, at the mercy of others, or dependent upon the bounty of a third portion, of those who hold its benefices. Let the State see to this—its union with it is *Siamese*, and one cannot suffer without the sympathy of the other —let us be paid; and let us be able, like other men, to support our families by the exercise of our calling, and not obliged to cut, and carve, and shuffle, either by editing newspapers, or writing such questionable works as this may seem to some, all for the means of gaining a simple livelihood.

CHAPTER XXII.

If WE had a religion, that consisted in absurd superstitions that had no regard to the perfection of our nature,
people might well be glad to have some part of their life
excused from it.

LAW.

THE melancholy catastrophe, which brought together
a scattered family, had been just preceded by the
arrival of my brothers from foreign climes; and we
were now concentrated upon this spot of the earth,
assigned, under heaven, to me and my family by the
Episcopal licence, to be had, held, and enjoyed,
upon a tenure which seems good (except in the event
of the incumbent's demise or the Bishop's veto) as
long as I have the conduct, means, and inclination to
make it availing. The eldest had been in almost
every country of Europe, and in many parts of the
new world; and having picked up, from his intermix-
ture with men of many religions as well as all

varieties of Christian discipline, a *melange* of ideas upon the subject, studied to profess a vast contempt for the ordinances of our religious establishment. The truth was, he would rather have no religion at all which placed any restraint upon men's actions; and, as the travelled philosopher finds fault with every thing pertaining to his own country, he brought the different forms of worship into a competition, by no means favourable to us, with the established forms of our church. At one time, the grandeur of the Latin church would inspire him with graphic recollections of the solemnity with which the Pope gave his blessing, from a balcony of the Vatican, to the prostrate multitude. At another, the blessing of the waters at St. Petersburgh, or the celebration of Easter-day, according to the ritual of the Greek church, would call his eloquence into action.

He would, at times, eulogize the stately solemnities of the Mahommedan worship, arguing, from the number of its votaries, in support of the respectability of their claims to universal proselytism. At times, the Jews' ancient creed would seem to triumph in his estimation, and, forgetting that he was thus paving the best and most orthodox way for the entrance of Christianity, he would impute to this, in defence of that, a mean dependence upon *the law and the prophets*. But, at the base of all these speculations, it was clear that Popery afforded the cherished mode of worship which he would embrace, had he really felt disposed to acknowledge (practically) the duty of religion. It had, to create his veneration, a sufficient antiquity; and the Holy Father, yet sitting in Peter's seat, had power enough over a poetic imagination to keep unnoticed the difference, so much vaster than the change of the circumstances of Christianity will warrant, between the unlettered, but inspired, fisherman of Galilee, and the sovereign of the Papal dominions surrounded with a brilliant court, relying upon the coffers of his treasury, protecting his interests by an army, and, in short, declaring, with all those mouths which speak the majesty of kings, MY *kingdom* IS *of* THIS *world.*

Besides, the religion of the Church of Rome had pageantry and procession, essentials so indispensable to the gratification of a taste which had led him to adopt the life of a military adventurer—the modern *knight-errant* whose " most disastrous chances"—whose " moving accidents by flood and field"—whose " hair-breadth 'scapes in th' imminent deadly breach" are all for a less substantial beauty, called *Liberty.* It had such an imposing effect upon the mind, with its vesper-bells and taper-lighted ceremonies—its cloistered monks and nuns were such ethereal representatives of our nature, so entirely bent on religious exercise, and wrapped up in adoration of their God. These godly maidens sang, too, such lovely hymns—witness, this account of the *Tourist*.

" To this celebrated place of pilgrimage (the church of Mariazell, in Upper Styria) many thousand good Catholics from Vienna and elsewhere annually repair, some in the honest hope of receiving blessings at the shrine of *a Madonna of St. Luke*, but more in that frame of mind which distinguished mine hoste of the Tabarde and his company in the Canterbury Tales. We met, however, with a pleasing hymn to the Virgin, sung by the young women at sunset as they slowly moved on their *knees round a sacred pillar*, and echoed by the men as they *bowed themselves to the earth before the image* it supported :—

' Fading, still fading, the last beam is shining,
Ave Maria! day is declining—
Safety and innocence fly with the light,
Temptation and danger walk forth with the night;
From the fall of the shade, till the matin shall chime,
Shield us from danger and save us from crime—
  Ave Maria! audi nos.

Ave Maria! hear when we call,
Mother of Him who is brother of all;
Feeble and failing we trust in thy might,
In doubting and darkness thy love is our light:
Let us sleep on thy breast while the night-taper burns,
And wake in thy arms when the morning returns—
  · Ave Maria! audi nos.' "

A tolerably strong indication that their adoration is not always directed to their God—unless this be a " woman whose name was Mary."

Is it not true, also, as he would ask, that linked with the Romish church stood every noble and soul-inspiring record of the past? Had not the kings and emperors of the world bent the knee, and thanked St. Peter's successor for their crowns? Were not all the glories of our own kingdom won, when our kings held their thrones at the mercy of another man? There was that, in the religion of Popery, which had such an irresistible effect upon the devotional faculties of our nature, that its very *perfumes* seemed the breath of heaven, and its veneration of images and relics of holy men, was admirably calculated to lead the feelings up to the supreme majesty of the Deity. Nay,—and the enthusiasm of my kinsman actually waxed to this height—the Pope, in his sacred habiliments, was no contemptible personification of the Almighty, while there was a solemnity in *his blessing* which brought to mind the excellence of eternal goodness, and made men, even in spite of their own wills, most devoted Christians.

To such flourishes it was my wont to listen, perhaps not calmly—for I had pride enough to feel, sometimes, the hues of indignation mount into my cheeks—but patiently; and then, when pauses permitted, I would reply with equal and, let us hope, more laudable zeal, in defence of our Protestant church, that all those ideal fascinations, which enslave the mind, are the greatest of the evils against which we *protest*—that it is that *passing* fervour of imagination which, being enthroned in the seat of that calm devotion which dwells in darkness and in solitude, is the unhealthy, the contaminating, the intoxicating element of *Papacy*. The reformers beheld all these enchantments, and exclaimed " Surely this is not the service acceptable to Him who must be worshipped ' *in spirit and in truth.*' God never meant his service to become a *pageant* or a *drama*, to amaze the eyes or affect the senses—there is no heart —no soul in this."

No, no ; man is prone to superstition—he loves it. But superstition is not Christianity ; neither is a hymn to the Virgin Mary any thing but an abomination to Him who declares—*I, the Lord, am one God, and there is none else.* As well might you exalt the morbid sensibility, which weeps at the recital of a stage-player, into that quality which more calmly sympathizes with the reality of suffering. How is it, that the noblest, most generous, most exalted mind is never so affected with the observation of actual grief, as that the tears, which cannot be restrained in the reading of a fiction, should reveal it? The benevolent *Howard* never thus betrayed his feeling when, face to face, the miseries of humanity approached him: but a far less benevolent—nay, a malevolent—man might be *forced to weep* at the *narrative* of ideal sufferings far less affecting.

There is a power, in the hands of man, of making impressions, I grant you; but they are not to be relied on for practical use. An exhibition of *puppets*, even, has more impression, of the *sentimental* kind, than a real view of the transactions, which they represent, would have had: and, if this be true, how vast is that power which is made up of all the aggregate properties of real performers—bodily stature, speech, aspect, gesticulation!

" Sheer sophistry!" would be the interjection; while I proceeded—Indeed, the very truth of this sophistry is evinced by your own declaration of the effects produced by the Pope and his benediction, in allusion to the Almighty and His attribute of goodness. Is it sober Christianity, that views, in a *man*, frail (at all events, as St. Peter, his assumed prototype and predecessor, if not) as ourselves, the personification of that BEING who " is *a Spirit*"—who is, in short, no more comparable to the figure of a man, than to that of a mountain, or to the impression on the mind which is made by *lightning* or its concomitant *thunder?* Much less, can a voice of a man convey to the mind, in a sober state, any notion of an eternal and unlimited extension of goodness to an universe of worlds. In a word, brother, it is *delusion* —it is a *phantasy* to which you ascribe the name of religion. How is it that we take up no book of *Tourist*, or *Traveller*, or *Sketcher*, who has made his way into Catholic countries, which does not discover to us the debasing effect of Popery? Here: suffer me to read this:—

" In proof of the gross superstition of the lower classes, I will relate a circumstance that has just occurred, and which occasions an excitement and an interest in Lisbon, which are almost incredible. At the distance of a few miles from hence is a certain field, in which a peasant boy was chasing a rabbit; the animal crept into an aperture in the side of a bank, closely followed by a dog; the boy, surprised to find that the latter did not return, determined to ascertain what had happened to prevent it, and accordingly groped his way into the bank, through the same narrow entrance; what was his astonishment, upon finding himself in a sort of cave, or hermitage, at the upper end of which he beheld an image of the Virgin! The discovery was soon made public, and the miracles affirmed to be worked by this image go on daily increasing; all ranks of persons are hastening to the spot, and it is asserted, among other popu-

lar tales, that when the boy first entered the cave, he
found both the rabbit and dog upon their knees, in
devout adoration of the image. A few days after the
opening of the shrine, this treasure unaccountably
disappeared, and an active search immediately com-
menced, which was happily terminated in the following manner :—

"A peasant was ploughing in the neighbouring
fields, when suddenly the oxen stood still; nor would
the sharpest application of the goad induce them to
move; the peasant, after vainly puzzling himself to
account for their obstinacy, chanced to cast his eyes
upon a tree overhead, whereon hung the identical
image, for whose recovery all hearts were anxious.
No sooner had he beheld the phænomenon, than the
animals began to turn round and around the tree, in
mystic dance, and completed the ceremony by falling
on their knees, like the rabbit and the dog !

" Every creature in Lisbon and its environs is
hastening to pay due adoration at the shrine of the
newly-discovered Virgin, who is about four inches
long, and being found, as I before mentioned, in a
cave near this place, is consequently denominated
' Nossa Senhora da Barracca ' (our lady of the cave).
Here, every evening, a friar descants upon the miracles said to have been performed by her; and a small
book, descriptive of them, has been published by

authority. The image is already covered with costly ornaments, among which are, a crown set with brilliants, and numerous gold chains; the gifts of those votaries who are able to afford such demonstration of their faith. An aged fidalga, and somewhat fanciful withal, living in this neighbourhood, and who has been bed-ridden for years past, has caused herself to be carried to the cave, and has, in consequence (as she declares), recovered the use of her limbs; the circumstance being well authenticated, affords additional proof of the extraordinary power of the imagination in nervous and hypochondriac complaints. The queen goes in grand state this evening, and makes an offering of a silver lamp. The field resembles an immense fair, and restaurateurs regularly attend in their booths, to provide for the refreshment of the company. Last night there were no less than thirty carriages upon the ground, and it is common to see more than a thousand of the peasantry and townspeople upon their knees, at one time surrounding the mouth of the cave. The friars have thought proper to declare, that a balsamic fragrance flows constantly from the image; and though there is always a strong smell of garlic and oil in the grotto, it is the fashion, upon entering, to exclaim, ' What a delicious odour!' I ought to tell you that the Senhora is not very easy of access, as the entrance of

her cave is so narrow, that persons are under the necessity of squeezing themselves in, creeping upon
their hands and knees, and the heat of the interior is
so insupportable, that several women have fainted.
All our household have, of course, been to pay their
devotions here.

"Since I wrote the above, one of the principal
leaders of the Constitution has made an attempt to
open the eyes of the multitude to the delusion of
Nossa Senhora da Barracca, and the Astro newspaper has written against it, but in vain; the leader
in question, notwithstanding his high official situation
actually received a box on the ear from the vigorous
arm of one of the fish-wives, who took offence at his
having uttered some expressions of contempt, when
he beheld the crowd kneeling before the door of the
cave. An unfortunate wag has also found reason to
repent the indulgence of his sarcastic humour; a
few days since, he tied an artificial hump upon his
shoulders, and going into the miraculous grotto, pre-
tended to come out again 'a straight and proper
man;' the circumstance was loudly celebrated, but
upon his imprudently shewing the trick he had
played, he was nearly torn to pieces by the populace,
and concluded by finding himself safely lodged in
the public prison. 'Our Lady,' in the meantime,
has been removed from the Barracca and conveyed

in solemn procession to one of the churches in Lisbon, where she is henceforth to take up her residence. She went by water, and was received upon the quay by a magnificent procession of priests, and a guard of honour. The concourse of people was immense. The government, it is said, have attempted to appropriate to their own use the treasures lavished by the devout upon this image. If so, it will only furnish an additional proof of their rash and incompetent judgment; true policy would never hazard a sudden overthrow of those superstitions which have been cherished as the realities of religion by the great mass of the people for so many ages past, and to which they are still so blindly prone.

" A counter-revolution was soon afterwards effected, and then the king, queen and royal family, accompanied by the ministers of state, paid their devotions at the shrine of Nossa Senhora da Barracca, the newly found image to whose benign interference the happy change was attributed. *Great is Diana of the Ephesians!*"—(Lisbon in 1821, 1822, and 1823. By Marianne Baillie, vol. ii. pp. 112. 128. 132.)

This, if true, was received only as the consequence of that ignorance common to the lower orders of all countries. But, is it not a proof, also, of the enslaving character of Popery—of its worldly wisdom—of its anti-christian domination? Imagine such a tissue of absurdities in Protestant England or Scotland (some such things may occur in Ireland)—in Protestant Germany or Switzerland—in Protestant America. The simple ghost-story is all the *leaven* which ever affects to work against the better judgment of the *poor* of these countries, *to whom the Gospel is preached.* In spite of bantering Infidelity, I went on:—As to the splendour and greatness which you seem to discover in connection with Popery, they are of the same kind, and, therefore, naturally agree with their great patroness. To the *purity* of the Christian Church such things have no more affinity, than the Gospel has to the immorality of the most bloody paganism. Is, or ought to be, the eye of *Christianity* more struck with the spectacle of a nation in arms than with the view of a flight of locusts? The splendour and greatness of true religion, and, therefore, of every thing connected with it, ought to be as fully developed in the wing of a beetle as in the imperial canopy of the greatest monarch—in the texture of a spider's web as in the intricacies of a forest—in the structure of a snail-shell as in the bulk of Vesuvius. God is infinite in all his works—each of them is infinite in perfection and beauty; and, strictly speaking, you make no nearer approaches to a knowledge of Him— a *spiritual*, mind, and *beneficial* knowledge of Him— whether you contemplate the minutest seed or a burning mountain. There is a vast difference; but it is not availing as that which will affect our knowledge of the invisible Maker of them both. The fact is, that we mix earthly with unearthly—carnal with spiritual things. We carry *these* bodies, with all their material appendages, into a world of *spirits,* and expect to understand these by means of those. Every religion, or form of religion, must labour under this disadvantage; but *Popery* is, of them all, more subject to, and most enthralled by it. Don't we speculate upon the mysteries of our faith, through the medium of our carnal minds? When you think of God making man, can you divest your mind, without an effort, of the idea of *hands* and *formation?* And why do not the same notions enter, when you contemplate the creation of *light?* Because one is *matter,* the other is not tangible. Carry, then, your thoughts, even one step higher, and let the mind gaze, with dazzled vision, upon the Maker of light. What says the Socinian? The Trinity is an absurdity, because our reason does not admit it. But, who, or what, tells him that we have a right here to know all those mysteries, the study of which is, probably, the intended pursuit of endless ages after death? The *worm* makes no inquiries—is not sceptical—upon the subject of *man,* denying the various branches of his intelligence, because it cannot comprehend them or him—because his acts and em-

ployments are altogether unaccountable and mysterious : but, I have yet to learn that there is more distance between the highest and lowest grade of the
animal scale, than between the Maker and the thing
made—the great God and fallen man—his creature.

In such a manner, would we wander away from
the subject at issue—he degenerating into political
considerations, I into pseudo-metaphysics, or sophis-
tries (as he called them); and so warm were we in
our respective arguments, that oftentimes the field
was, by common consent, or, at the instigation of the
hearers, abandoned by both combatants; and finally
we agreed that, after his departure, (until which the
subject was never to be revived) we should corres-
pond upon it by letter. He was to open fire, and we
shall arrive at his first epistle in due time—It came
along with an exquisite painting, by himself, of the
Incarnate Saviour after his resurrection.

CHAPTER XXIII.

I speak as my understanding instructs me, and as
mine honesty puts it to utterance.

SHAKSPEARE.

MEANWHILE the affairs of the curate went on much
in the accustomed style.* By little and little incum-
brances were removed; the wolf was kept from entering, though he frequently showed his teeth at the
door.

I have, in a former place, awarded to myself an
eulogium, on the pains which I bestowed upon the
public ministrations connected with my office; and
every day bears testimony to the real opportunities
which a clergyman has, herein, of rightly expounding
the word of God, shining, as it does, throughout the

* While correcting these pages, the author is too happy to
embrace every opportunity of withdrawing *apparent* spleen to
allow him to omit saying, in this place, that, since the removal of
two or three boys from the grammar-school, there has been a
vast improvement in the public conduct of the present number
—still, however, they put out the candles at church.

whole of our Liturgy. Alas! how commonly is our service reduced to a mere formality, for want of endeavouring to feel, while we read its various parts ; and how true it is, that, if the congregation is to feel their edifying tendency, he who ministers must not only feel, but show that he feels, the import of every word he utters. Any thing theatrical is perfectly unessential to this ; much more, any thing studied or affected —it must be the result of *real feeling*.

Who, for instance, would not be in danger of overlooking the manifold exhortations of Scripture to *an acknowledgment and confession of sins*, were the minister to say—" the Scripture moveth us, in sundry places to acknowledge and confess,"—instead of— " in sundry places, to acknowledge and confess ?"— The former is obviously applicable to the variety of *places of worship*. And, lower down, in the same opening address, where the intention is to invite the hearers to let this *acknowledgment and confession* run through *all their dovotions,* it may be completely nullified by that common *stop* after " when we assemble and meet together," and the sense appear to be this, that " we ought most chiefly *so* to do—to render thanks, &c., when we assemble and meet together."

Then, again, in the " general confession," this admission is, I am afraid often, made—" We have followed too much the devices and desires of our *own* hearts ;" whereas the emphatic word is the last—that natural fountain out of which proceed all the evils of man's conversation in the world.

Much skill is required in pronouncing " the Absolution of Sins" by " ALMIGHTY GOD," to bring down the force of these august words properly, to " He pardoneth, &c. ;" and, perhaps, the best way is, if I may use the word, to *slur* the pronoun *he*, which is certainly *not* emphatic, being inserted only on account of the distance between the verb and its *nominative*.

May I presume to make a remark upon the reading of " the Lord's Prayer," I will only say to the despiser of these comments, if but one young clergyman should be induced, hereby, to cultivate a true style of reading (not my style), think what incalculable benefit may accrue to the community—how many congregations, the unlettered members of which require the plain sense of every passage to be stated in the plainest manner—so different is even the most ordinary phrase from their common mode of speech,—may be enlightened or confounded by the minister's mode of delivery—how their children's children may be influenced by *their* understanding of the Liturgy !

" Give us this *day,* our daily *bread,*" is, undeniably, the common way in which lisping infancy is taught to pray for *sufficient for the time being* of all those things of which we stand in need : but is not *this* a more appropriate way — " Give us, *this* day, our *daily*-bread "—*Bestow upon us, now, according to thy wonted grace, the supply of all our present wants?*

Every churchman knows that our service contains many ascriptions of " glory"—" as it was" yesterday, " is" to-day, and, " shall be" for ever—to the three persons of the *triune Jehovah*, in the same form of words ; and, therefore, the importance of giving these aright is evidently great. But, owing, either to the punctuation, which, here as throughout the Psalms, and in the *Te Deum*, is nothing more than a direction to the *choristers*, where the service is chaunted, or to the *cacoethes* of Parish-clerks—not to venture to say *some* of the clergy—how commonly is the whole devotion of a grand passage destroyed ! Instead of—

Glory be to the Father; and to the Son; and to the Holy Ghost.

As it was in the beginning; is now and ever shall
    be; world without end, Amen—
as it is too commonly said, shall we not endeavour to restore the meaning, even though better men should appear to be the subjects of our animadversion, by reading, as we have the opportunity, thus :—

" Glory be—to the Father, and to the Son, and to the Holy Ghost,

" As—it *was* in the beginning, *is* now, and *ever shall be* world without end. Amen." ?

And let not the minister omit to say his own *Amen*, either here, or at the end of the Lord's Prayer, or after the general confession, or after every form of our creed. The *italics*, in the common Prayer Book, will show when this is to be said by the people *only ;* and it should never be forgotten that the minister sometimes joins in prayer *with* the congregation, and sometimes presents, *for* them, to Almighty God, prayers to which they convey their assent by saying *Amen*. One would think the clergy had borrowed, from the conventicle, the practice of leaving this delightful ejaculation to the people.

The *Te Deum* is the next part of our service which comes under observation ; and it must be confessed, that the force and devotion of this truly scriptural Hymn—retained from the earliest ages of the Christian church—are nearly lost by the practice of reading it *alternis carminibus.*

Much, however, may be done by the care and (so to speak) contrivance of the *minister*, which it is perhaps, hopeless to expect from the generality of parish-clerks.

When the clerk and people have said (as they ought to say)

" To thee cherubin and seraphin continually do
   cry —"

it has always been my endeavour to subjoin quickly,
or, rather, *unintermittedly*, and in a tone which may
convey the unfinished state of what has been said,

" Holy, holy, holy, Lord God of Sabaoth !"—
without that affectation of the Hebrew peculiarities
of the final word, which, in my ears, always sounds
pedantic, and sometimes offensive.

   Again, when it has been said—

" The holy church, throughout all the world, doth
   acknowledge thee —"

surely the sense is not complete.   The acknowledgment intended is, that the *Lord God* is, individually and collectively, according to the sacred
doctrine of the Trinity in Unity, the three Persons
respectively announced in the three succeeding verses;
and, consequently, the same endeavour should be
made as in the last instance.   The whole remaining
part of the *hymn*, I have always considered to be
addressed to *God the Saviour*, in the *person* of our
Lord Jesus Christ.

   Before we leave this part of our subject, it may be
observed, that the opinion of him who here ventures to
offer his sentiments is, that the *Te Deum* can only be
restored to its original effectiveness by letting it be
" said or sung" by the minister and people together,

or, as the *creeds* are, the minister leading and the people following. There is nothing, in the directions of the Rubrick, which gives any claim to the common method, but, rather, the reverse; and, therefore, a charge of innovation could not rest against the change; while, for my part, what I learned in infancy is even now, in this matter, a good and lasting piece of wisdom—*sera nunquam est ad bonos mores via.* And may I ask, why is not the splendid *canticle*, appointed to be used, *ad libitum*, in place of the *Te Deum*, at least now and then, resorted to? I have used it once or twice; but general practice seems to condemn me. It would, I think, relieve the *sameness*, sometimes objected to our Liturgy. The like option is given in the service after the second lesson, but as generally declined. Surely no one will say, *the shorter is preferable.*

The Apostles' Creed every child is taught to repeat; but, if mothers and teachers will stoop to receive a word of counsel, let me make a remark or two upon the usual methods which, though *erroneous* and calculated to occasion *error*, not unfrequently follow us from the nursery to the public assembly of the church.

In the article " *Suffered, under Pontius Pilate,*" &c. great stress is commonly laid upon *Pontius Pilate;* but, *suffered* is the emphatic word, the three other words embracing a *fact* which, though essential, is subordinate.

" *Was crucified, dead, and buried,*" is often hurried over, as if expressive of *one* event only; and with a carelessness which seems to forget that hereby we confess our belief that JESUS not only was affixed to the cross, but that he *died* on the cross in consequence of pain and agony, and that, as a conclusive evidence of his death, he *was buried*. He is the Saviour, " *who*"—was " *crucified,*" *was* " *dead,*" " *and* " *was* " *buried.*"

" *The third day he rose again from the dead,*" if rightly understood, will carry to the mind the conviction of *three* most important facts—

1st. That the " *hell,*" into which our Lord " descended," is the abode of " the dead ;"

2nd. That from this place " he *rose* again,"— not " rose *again,*" or a *second* time ;

3rd. That this resurrection took place (not on the third *day,*) but " on the *third* day," in fulfilment of all the prophecies to this effect.

Whatever merit may belong to the next remark is due to an excellent little work, by Bishop Mant— " The Clergyman's Obligations," from which indeed, I have derived many of those hints which I am now presuming to deal out *second-hand*.

The last of the three *paragraphs,* into which this

creed is divided in reference to the Three Persons of the Godhead, is usually repeated in three distinct clauses; thus, " I believe in the Holy Ghost, the Holy Catholic Church;—The Communion of Saints, the Forgiveness of Sins;—The Resurrection of the Body, and the Life Everlasting, Amen;"—than which nothing can be more glaringly improper.

Either *five* distinct articles, notwithstanding the common punctuation, are hereby confounded in *three* couplets; or, allowing that, if they were *six*, they might, without much harm, go together in couples, the *second* article is cut in halves between the *first* and the *second* couplet. The *articles* are :—

1st, (I believe in) the Holy Ghost;

2d, ————— the Holy Catholic Church—the Communion of Saints;

3d, ————— the Forgiveness of Sins;

4th, ————— the Resurrection of the Body;

5th, ————— the Life Everlasting;

and the *Amen* conveys an unfeigned assent to the *whole Creed.*

We must, then, in obedience to the right reverend prelate's advice, have it read thus :—

" I believe in—*the Holy Ghost; the Holy Catholic Church—the Communion of Saints; the Forgiveness of Sins; the Resurrection of the Body; and, the Life Everlasting. Amen* " — and yet I never heard it read so in all my life. Surely, it is not orthodox to adhere to bad practices; for that must be bad which has a tendency to mislead the people, and give them vague suspicions about *the saints* in the Romish Calendar, when *the Communion of Saints* is synonymous with, and explanatory of, the other expression —*the Holy Catholic Church.*

In "the second collect," the close affinity by which "who," "of whom," and "whose," are bound together in reference to "O GOD," cannot be overlooked without debilitating a very beautiful form of prayer: as, in "the third collect," there is a connection, which should not be lost sight of, between "to the beginning of this day," and "in the same."

Omitting the prayers not used in the morning of the Sabbath and other Litany-days, we pass now to "the Litany"—a form of words which cannot be surpassed for purity, for universality, for comprehensiveness, for accordance to Scripture, for unity of spirit. The observations which I have seen, we will not note; but those which I have *not seen* only, lest I should seem to point out well-known ways, shall now be offered to the reader. Let him not despise me; my intention is to do good.

When the *minister* prays unto the Lord, for himself and in behalf of his flock,—"be not angry with us for ever," is it to be understood that the *continued* anger of the Almighty is deprecated, or, that the spirit of the petition is that he will *never be angry with us?* I think the latter, and am fortified in my opinion by the reflection that " if his wrath be kindled, (yea, but a little,) blessed are all they that put their trust in him." (Psalm ii. 12.)

Schism is usually pronounced *scism,* with the *c* soft; but, I think, improperly. *Usage* may be allowed some deference, as our different pronunciation of *scheme,* and *schedule,* seems to demand; but no other word, but this *schism,* is allowed to deny its Greek parentage altogether.

The petition—" That it may please thee to give to all thy people increase of grace to hear, &c." requires an effort in order to its proper delivery. There should not be any pause after *grace;* but, in order that the voice may be prepared to go on, let the syllables *increase* be uttered slowly and in a suspended tone.

" That it may please thee to preserve all that travel by land or by water "—ought to have a comma after *travel.*

In the last petition, beginning with " That it may," and in the last part of it, I should recommend, in order that the sense may be felt, a pause after *grace,* and also after *spirit;* thus, " endue us with the grace —of thy Holy Spirit—to amend," &c.

The *monotony* of all these petitions, which are

couched in the same style of language, will be greatly relieved, as will the tendency to weary be generally weakened, by a variation in the emphasis of the minister: and, of the words " *that it may please,*" the first, third, or fourth may have the *ictus* with good effect. Some of them, too, will admit a very forcible stress upon the next word—"*thee,*" where the blessing prayed-for is eminently of such a character as to be in the gift of *God only.*

In the supplication—" *O Lord, deal not with us after our sins,*" as well as that which follows by the people, it would be very desirable to give the force and meaning of the word *after—according to.* This, I think, can only be effected by avoiding the common stress upon the word, and giving an uniform emphasis to the last two words—*our sins—our iniquities.*

After the succeeding invitation to silent and heart-felt prayer, the minister offers up a most beautiful petition, which, however, according to the reading of it, may be variously understood. Should he pause after the word *despisest,* an idea may be conveyed that the *Almighty* does despise some things; which, however correct, appears not to be the meaning. The pause, it seems, should be after *not.* Again, to what do the words—*whensoever they oppress us*—apply? to *prayers,* or to *troubles and adversities?* I think, to the former. I should say also, that the semicolon,

usually after *oppress us,* would be better after *hear us;*
so that we may have a supplication for the *divine
assistance* and a *gracious hearing* in behalf of our
labouring prayers—" Mercifully assist our *prayers,*
that we make before thee in all our troubles and
adversities, *whensoever* they *oppress* us, and graciously
hear us; that," &c.

In the prayer for the Parliament, let the words—
as for this kingdom in general, so especially—be given
in a *parenthetic* tone, that the main current may run
on from *we humbly beseech thee* to *for the High Court
of Parliament.* And, how often do we hear the succeeding part of this prayer read in a manner destruc-
tive of its sense. It cannot be that we pray to God
" to direct and prosper *all* their consultations," so
that they may tend " to the advancement of his
glory," &c.; but, certainly, only such of them as
have this tendency. It is a long passage, and requires
some management. I read it thus; " That thou
wouldest be pleased to direct and prosper—all their
consultations to—the advancement of *thy* glory, the
good of thy *Church,* the safety, honour, and welfare
of *our Sovereign* and his *dominions."* And, in the
prayer instead of the Litany, how often do we hear a
petition that " the good estate of the Catholic Church "
may be " guided and governed " by HIS " *good*
Spirit," as if our Maker had also an *evil* Spirit.

In the rehearsal of the Ten Commandments, it is, perhaps, surprising how much may be done towards the proper effect of this ceremony, by an attention to their real spirit and meaning.

The *first,* with the short preamble, is strikingly impressive; but a careless reader has it in his power to defeat the impression. GOD should be uttered with reverence, clearly, and audibly to the whole congregation, and succeeded by a short pause indicative of the reflection that *these words* do not emanate from the wisdom of man—" *spake these words,*" should follow firmly, slowly, and equably, while the following " *and said* " may properly be read with a suppressed voice. Then, *I am the Lord thy God* with nerve and solemnity, not in imitation of, but befitting the simple and tremendous statement of, the Creator who thus demands the homage of his rational subjects. When schoolboys, we invariably hurried over the remainder — *Thou shalt have none other gods but* ME —with fearful rapidity, as if afraid of losing that power of emphasis reserved for the final *me:* but this is, perhaps, the only word which does *not* require an emphasis, the preceding declaration having, more powerfully than any other could have, challenged the honour due to God *alone.*

The *second,* it is a pity, is much injured by the full stop after *under the earth;* and he, who should read it accordingly, would convey to the ignorant an idea that the *making* of images or likenesses is, in itself, prohibited ; whereas God commanded several of these to be made even in the construction of the tabernacle. *Thou shalt not bow down to them, nor worship them,* should follow, after a suspension, rather than a cessation of voice, and be read with clearness and precision. *Here* should be the full stop ; for here, and not before, the commandment is terminated.

In the third, there should be no stop after *guiltless,* unless also after *him.*

" Remember that thou keep holy the Sabbath-*day*" —may do in the nursery ; but let those who have put away childish things, temporally at all events, give the stress to *Sabbath*—No one would say " the Rest-*day.*" I have heard it said—" In it thou shalt do *no manner* of work ;" surely it should be,—" no manner of *work*," an emphasis which would greatly distinguish between the *necessary,* or good works of the New Testament, and those daily tasks by which a man earns his livelihood. A due observance of the accent on *hállowed* is necessary to avoid the danger of falling into the pronunciation *hallowéd it,* which is not uncommon. Indeed, the whole of the last clause requires attention—" *Wherefore (in consideration of* WHICH)—the Lord *blessed* the *seventh day (day* now requires an emphasis as well as *seventh,* to shew that

God .vouchsafed his blessing even upon the *day* of His rest)—and *hallowed* it."

The *fifth* commandment is sometimes read just as it is *stopped*; but, would it not be better to make the *comma* after the word *long*? Do not read "*may belong*" for "*may-be long.*"

In the *sixth*, to say—*Thou shalt do—no murder—*(as, as far as I know, it is invariably said) certainly involves a grammatical absurdity, enjoining the *doing* of that which is either *not done* or *not to be done.* Much more effective, as well correct, would be *Thou shalt do no—*MURDER; and thus, this prohibition would fall into the train of those which follow :—

  VI. *Thou shalt do no*   -   MURDER.

  VII. *Thou shalt not commit* ADULTERY.

  VIII. *Thou shalt not* - -   STEAL.

  IX. *Thou shalt not*   - -   BEAR FALSE WITNESS.

  X. *Thou shalt not*   - -   COVET.

Who has not heard, in the *ninth*, a great stress laid on *against* and *neighbour?* But the emphatic part of the prohibition is all involved in the portion contained in the Diagram above. Of the *tenth*, I shall only observe that *any* is a word which requires *stress.*

In the delivery of the *Creed* following, the reader may learn much from the little book by the bishop already mentioned; but yet I am prone to say a word or two, if his patience be not quite exhausted.

By whom all things were made should be read so as *not* to be concluded with *with the Father ;* for it is attributed here to *the Son,* agreeably with the declaration of St. John that " all things were made by him." (i. 3.) Neither should *whose kingdom shall have no end* be connected with *the dead,* or with even *both the quick and the dead,* for a reason equally strong and cogent.

The danger of falling into this latter fault may be, in some measure, obviated, by a proper delivery of the awful truth embraced in the foregoing declaration— *And* HE *shall come* AGAIN, WITH GLORY, *to* JUDGE *both the quick and the dead,* in which a stop should be after *again,* and another after *glory.*

The learned Bishop of Down and Connor recommends, in saying *The Lord and Giver of life,* a stop after *Lord ;* arguing that this word implies the *Deity* of the third Person in the Trinity, and not that He is the *Lord of life,* as well as the *Giver of life,* which would certainly be redundant.

I should have now closed this chapter, and with it this subject, but for an observation which appears to me of sufficient moment to warrant one more *draught* upon the reader's *endurance.* The prayer, very commonly selected for the pulpit before the sermon, is the Collect for the second Sunday in Advent, and one of its passages is not unfrequently read— *that, by pa-*

tience and comfort of thy holy Word, we may, &c., when the Epistle which follows the collect clearly shows that it cannot mean—*by patience* (as well as *by comfort) of the Word of God,* unless it is to be proved that *a patient endurance* of the *Word of God* is more likely to be meant than *a patient endurance* of *all the afflictions* by which it pleaseth Him to *try* or *chasten* us in this probationary state of being.

END OF VOL. I.

PRINTED BY STEWART AND CO., 15, OLD BAILEY.

CPSIA information can be obtained
at www.ICGtesting.com
Printed in the USA
BVHW08s1032210918
528173BV00022B/1196/P

9 781330 881620